I0158641

THERE BE DRAGONS

MARIANNE SIMON

There Be Dragons
Text copyright © 2025 Marianne Simon

All rights reserved. No part of this publication may be reproduced, distributed, or transmitted in any form or by any means, including photocopying, recording, or other electronic or mechanical methods, without the prior written permission of the author, except in the case of brief quotations embodied in critical reviews and certain other noncommercial uses permitted by copyright law.

For permission requests, please contact:
https://www.mariannebecoming.com

Cover and interior design by MuzammilFaarooq

Paperback ISBN: 978-1-7321436-1-6
Ebook ISBN: 978-1-7321436-2-3

CONTENTS

FORWARD

W elcome. I am honored you are here.

If you are reading these words, it is likely you have tasted loss, your own version of it. The end of a relationship, the loss of a home, a dream that has died, or the ferocious loss of a beloved that blindsides you, leaving you forever changed.

> Perhaps you're standing at the edge.
> Perhaps you've fallen off and wonder how you will survive.
> Perhaps you are finding your way to a new becoming.

On May 8, 2017, my husband of 26 years went in for a simple surgery and never came home.

That day changed the trajectory of my life. As I travelled each painful step forward without him, the biggest lesson I learned was I had to do it my own way and in my own time.

Today I can claim joy, delight, renewed purpose. Yet there are days I still gasp at how much I miss him.

I started writing about this journey the day after he died, and I am still writing it. It is a collection of poetry, personal stories, and metaphor that serve as a reminder that even when everything falls apart, we are still held. And that even from the farthest edge… there is a way home.

The title to the book, "There Be Dragons," came to me years ago. Why dragons? Because I was intrigued by the old belief that the world was flat and when we sailed to the edge of it, we would fall off. There, in the depths would be dragons waiting to devour us.

But what I discovered was that though the drop was beyond terrifying, the dragon herself was not to be feared. Quite the opposite, she was there as protector, healer, source of inner wisdom, courage and power.

My great hope is that these writings will bring you comfort and permission to travel this time in your own unique way. Listening to your soul's wisdom to guide your forward.

To your journey.
Marianne

WHAT FAIRY TALE?

Once upon a time, there was a girl who met a boy. They got married and had a daughter and lived happily, give or take, for a long time. Then one day, in the middle of May, he went to the hospital for a simple procedure and never came home again.

And she was left to pick up the pieces.

There was no fairytale ending to help her understand what happened. She would have to figure it out for herself.

Years later, looking back at the rest of that story, I could never have told you how that road would unfold. I could never have guessed how long and how deeply I would mourn. I could never have known, even when we were married, how much I loved him and how much I would miss him. It was a strange comfort to learn I loved him so very much.

It was a wonder I got through it, though that term 'getting through it' is not right. As though it were an exam to be passed or a rough day at work. It was more like I kept moving into the future, shedding skin. Evolving, continually evolving, until it no longer hurt quite so much. And I found that somehow, I had indeed stepped myself into a different life.

In the beginning, the destination was a moving target. It was simply the next breath, the next meal, the next morning, the next night. It was letting friends and family know what happened. Listening to calls, reading notes, all full of condolences that did nothing to ease the pain, but were appreciated.

There were the logistics to be dealt with, the funeral arrangements, the memorial, the obituary, the financials. Calling social security, pension funds, life insurance. Because even as the grief tore me apart, I was terrified as to how I would pay the bills.

In all of that was the wish upon a star, the prayer, the begging, that just on the other side, it wouldn't hurt quite so much.

It was a bit like climbing a mountain. Each time, coming around a bend, thinking I would be a little further along, a little closer to the top, only to look down and see I was in nearly the same place.

Eventually, and not in a straight line, but rather in a fast forward, time-warp kind of way, I found myself in some facsimile of 'normal.' But it was all so strange. Going out with friends and noting the obvious empty chair at the table. Heading back to work, with the looks and questions that left me feeling exposed and raw. Even at the farmer's market, having the vendor ask where the husband was, breaking down as I answered, "He's gone."

And in all of that, were the surprises. Going to *Hamilton* and discovering that for 90 minutes I was not consumed by loss. Laughing at a story. Waking up, putting on my slippers, and thinking, "Oh. He is not the very first thing I thought about this morning."

With that came the inevitable guilt. How could I laugh? How could I find pleasure? How could I find contentment without him?

But most likely this is not your story. Not your experience at all. I found when my mother passed away at 91 after a long illness, my sister and I caring for her 24/7 during the heart of the pandemic, it was a very different grieving process.

None of it is wrong, none of it is too slow or too fast. It is each person's timeline, journey, unfolding.

Today I stand on the mountain and the view is different.

Many times, we can't see the distance we've come when we're in it, foot stumbling over foot. But at some point, in some strange distant future, when we look out we discover we are no longer where we were before.

Along the way, we figure some things out. We uncover a path. If we give ourselves the time and space to listen to our intuition, to surrender to our deepest needs, we find our way.

To Mike

my lark

*In the beginning, there
was so much love.*

LEAF MIST

C lose your eyes. Now, slowly open them and watch the mist on the leaf. For you see, all leaves breathe. They call it transpiration. It is nearly invisible to the naked eye. The leaves open their stomata, filling their cells with carbon dioxide, and with a very slow exhale, they release oxygen back into the air.

If you open your eyes and look, oh, so carefully, you will see the faintest of mists rising from the leaf. You will have to be patient, and you will have to breathe very carefully, or you will disturb the pattern of the mist.

I think seven-year-old girls are the very best at watching leaves breathe. They can sit perfectly in the moment, concentration locked on. The softest, smallest of breaths, as they watch.

That is where children breathe, onto your cheek.

And it is into the crook of the neck that lovers breathe. In their breath, you smell their scent and yours mingling, as the warm air rises to your nostrils.

That is where I breathe, into the crook of your neck. Where the tip of my nose rubs up against the bristles of your chin. And I smell my toothpaste and your soap.

In that crook of your neck, I find sanctuary and solace. And in the taste of your skin, I find the sea.

I close my eyes as your arms wrap me tight. My head reaching your cheekbone, my chest against yours. And I breathe you in.

As atom by atom, I find you.

Then, one day, the man went into the hospital for a simple surgery .... And never came home.

May 8, 2017

3:15 pm.

With that, she fell off the edge of the world.

This is the tale of her journey as she found her way

To a new story.
A different story.
The story of her own becoming.

SHATTERING

There are no words.
And yet words are all I have.

STUNNED HEART

Into the freezer.
Hit me with the numb gun.
Safer there.

No thoughts there.
Time is frozen there.

No moment after.
No walk down the hall.
No sitting in the chair.
No looks of sorrow and dismay.

No, "I'm sorry, so sorry.
I'm sorry, so very, very sorry."

My heart is stunned, frozen.

Don't take me there.
Don't say the words.
Don't take my hands.
Don't say the words.

Then perhaps it won't be true.

And I can take these past few weeks out of deep freeze,
And go on
As if nothing has changed.

NO ONE HOME

There is no one home.
    Do not come knocking today.

The curtains are drawn,
        The door is locked.
        Do not coming knocking today.

Can you hear me from outside?
        I have the music turned up loud
        To muffle the sounds.

Under the pounding of the drums,
        The railing of the guitar,
        Can you hear my cries?

Holding the pillow tight to my chest.
        Do I imagine it is him I am holding so tightly,
        Squeezing like breath?

I rock on the bed,
        Swallow the corner of the pillow
        To gag the sounds,
        Gag the pain.

Do not coming knocking today.
        There is no cheerful smile.
        No bright hello.
        No "Thanks for coming by."

The eyes are closed.
    The windows sealed.
    The blinds tightly turned.

Please don't come knocking at the door.
    Can't you read the "Do Not Disturb" sign?
    The "Do Not Ring."

No one is home.
    No one you'd want to meet.
    Straggling to the door,
    Eyes swollen,
    Nose running,
    Don't make me pretend you are welcome.

What more signs do you need?
    I am not home.
    To knocks and rings,
    Questions and calls,
    Texts and concerns.

Let me lick my wounds,
    Curl up in the blanket,
    Suck my thumb, if I could.

At last.
    The knocking stops.
    The rings end.

I am left alone with the grief.

Hurricane Season

It is rising. I feel it rising.
What do I do with the rising?
This bellowing cauldron
Of rising emotions
That have no outlet.

Hurricane winds and tsunami waves
That swirl and beat against chest and belly, thighs and mouth
Seeking out,
Out. Out.

Can relief be found in fists on flesh?
On feet pounding ground?
Tossing the cat through the window?
Throwing the baby over the sill?

This is where the monsters come from.
This, with nails and fangs
And bulging eyes and wild hair
That we pull at,
Because our hands can't stop shaking.

Again and again, crying and screaming
Into the howling winds.
How could you?
Why would you?
How could you
Leave me?

Unleash it.

Throw open the doors and windows
To the ripping, roaring,
Flatten the trees
Fury, that wants her out.

They don't tell us what to do with this part.
How to manage, corral, release, ride this part.
We are not taught to ride the hurricane.

There is no logic in this place.
No rational thought in this place.
It is the brew cooked way too long.

Kick something,
Throw something,
Tear something,
Slam something,
Break something,
Crash something,
Smash something,
Into a million billion pieces.

Because that is how it feels inside.
The million billion shards
That tear and shred from the inside out.
That gut my belly,
Choke my throat,
Leave me dizzy and frenzied
With no place to go.

Will they call the doctor?
Bring relief, release, with white pills
Or blue pills or amber liquid.

Put me in a padded cell.

To quiet it, dampen it, put it back to sleep.
Trap it, still it, stuff it.
Shut it the fuck up.

No platitudes, please.
No "There, there."
No "It will be ok."
Not now.
Not right now.
It will not be ok.

So go.
I just need to go.
To the sea
To the sand
To dance
To run
To shriek
Banshee wild woman shriek.

It's where the monsters come from.
We give them shape and features,
But it's where they come from.

I look in the mirror
And can't quite believe what I see.
A woman with blue eyes, soft lips,
Brown curly hair.

That can't be what she looks like.
It certainly isn't what she feels like.
She should look like a monster.
She feels like a monster.
Hurts like a monster.

I have to put the cat out for his own protection.
Ask my sister to watch the babe for her own protection.
I am not safe to be around during hurricane season.
When the monster comes out to feed.

ANGELS EVERYWHERE

It was just after my husband Mike died and I was on the Santa Monica boardwalk making a slow trudge towards the pier. In my numbed stupor, I literally watched my feet as I took one step and then another. My body feeling as if it belonged to someone else. In the first few days right after his death, I hadn't been able to get further than a block or two without gasping for breath. Yet, for the first time on this bright spring morning, there was an odd satisfaction I had come as far as I had.

As I neared the pier, I noticed a homeless man in a bright blue poncho sitting on a bench, dozing. He had a large cardboard sign next to him:

Rescue Me
Help $ or Hugs

I walked past him and then stopped, looking back. Maybe it was the words, "Rescue Me" that called, but I turned around and went back to sit next to him on the bench.

"Hello," I whispered, as he shook himself awake. "I don't have any money." Pause. "Would you like a hug?"

He was alert now, staring at me. I imagine he was rather surprised at this odd woman sitting down next to him, offering him a hug. He was an older gentleman, dark skin, with graying hair, and one eye that looked off in a slightly different direction than the other. Next to him were a couple of plastic bags filled with clothes and that sign. He looked around before nodding yes, and I reached over and awkwardly gave him a hug.

Then he asked the question, "How are you today?"

Boom! Couldn't pretend otherwise. "Not so good," I answered, "Not so good."

My lips quivered and the tears flowed as I shared how my husband had just passed away. And then there he was, taking my hand, whispering words of consolation. Telling me that Mike was in a better place now, that God had called him home. I cried even harder.

Together we rocked back and forth on that bench. At one point, he asked me to please stop crying, he was worried the police would come by and think he was hurting me.

Eventually, the tears stopped, and we sat together on that bench, my small hand in his larger calloused one. I told him a bit about Mike and our marriage, our adventures and travels. It was a relief to share some of the sweet times.

My new friend's name was Merle, and he delighted in the fact that all three of our names began with an 'M.' He told me about his brothers and how they'd all been born on holidays: 4th of July, Christmas Day, New Year's Eve. He shared how someone had stolen his bike, his pack, his identification. It was a tough place out there.

Merle was a religious man. He believed in God. He told me that Mike was right there, watching out for me. Even as the tears welled, I laughed when he joked that Mike might not take it kindly that he was hugging me so much, this stranger on a bench.

I could feel the shift in our connection as the time came to say goodbye. I eased my hand out of his strong warm ones, moved just a little further away on the bench.

"Thank you." I said, from the depths of my heart.

"Thank you." He answered, from the love in his.

At any other time, I couldn't imagine myself acting this way, getting so close, sharing so vulnerably with a stranger. My old prejudices and fears were so strongly ingrained. But on this day, during this time of great need, that wall came down, those fears merely an illusion.

There is much goodness in the world. In that time together, we were not strangers, he, a homeless man, me, a recent widow. We were two souls both in need of comforting who found each other on a park bench.

His beautiful eyes sparkled as he took my hands one last time. "Blessings," he said, before he kissed them and let me go.

There are angels everywhere.

YOU ARE THE OBSTACLE COURSE I AVOID

You are the obstacle course I avoid.
The detour I make.
The abyss I elude.

Because it hurts so much to think of you,
and to not think of you.
I haven't figured that out yet.
    I'm afraid you are in a place of limbo.

I sit here this morning writing about the things I am working
on. Projects and plans I am starting to look forward to. I am
aware that change keeps rolling on regardless of what I want.

Although, each morning I wake up and you are still not here.
That has not changed.

There are times now, sometimes long, sometimes short, when it feels 'normal.'
I have my to-do lists, my appointments, my chores.
My outings and pleasures.
I smile. I laugh.
I even mean it sometimes.

But as I go about my day, making my plans, filling out my calendar, it strikes
me that missing you is trapped in my body.
All the time.

Even if I'm not thinking of you, my missing you lives in
    My clenched jaw,
    My aching shoulders,
    My cramped belly,
    My thudding head,
    My ramrod back,
    My tight throat,
    My panting breaths.

I take a deep, deep breath. Stretch my arms. Shake my hips. Twist my spine.
Not to shift you out of my life, but rather to find a way to
move forward with a bit more space, a bit more ease.

There is no choice I'm afraid. No alternate route.

In my mind, I take your arm the way I used to and whisper, "My
love, will you walk with me? Will you help me ease the way?"

You look at me the way you always did. Pulling my arm in
a little closer, giving me a bite of your ice cream sandwich
and nodding, "Of course, my dearest. Always."

30 Pieces of Silver

Mike was a carpenter. He loved doing projects around the house, especially woodworking. His favorite pastime was making things, our bed frame, a 'window' between the kitchen and the pantry, my jewelry box. I was always impressed by the time and care he took with the details; it was his form of creative expression.

A few months after he died, I sold his tools.

Not all of them, but the big ones, the ones I would never use. On impulse, riding a wave of making space and claiming the house as mine, I put two up for sale. Within an hour there were three inquiries. They were priced to sell, I was not interested in haggling; simply wanted them out of the garage so I could free up some room.

A fellow came that evening, tall and lanky. He and his roommate, an architect, didn't know much, but wanted to create a woodshop in their garage; these tools would make a great start.

"Can we turn them on?" He asked, as he sized up the chop saw. I wasn't sure how, these were Mike's tools. But between us we plugged it in and found the switch. As the motor roared to life the lights in the garage flickered. "Looks like it works." Yup.

The other item was an old table saw Mike had brought out from Ohio. It was a bit rusted, nothing fancy. There was a guide for the wood, and you could angle the blade to get a mitered cut. Ah, I remembered something from woodshop in college after all. It too, roared to life when we flipped the switch. Mike took care of his tools.

"Would you take $75 for the two?" Sure, I nodded. I had originally thought to donate them, so this was more than I'd considered. Except my stomach clenched.

"Anything else?" He asked. I looked around, there was a router in the corner. I was never going to use a router.

"You can have that if you want." He flipped it on, making sure it worked. Yup.

"Do you have any wood?" It started feeling like vultures circling. But yes, for $100 they could take the chop saw, the table saw, the router and the wood. I would not be using them.

They loaded up the van, then handed over the bills. I didn't bother counting them. But as they drove off into the night I suddenly panicked. Wait! I wanted to shout at them.

> Stop! Wait, I've changed my mind.
> Bring it back.
> You can't have that.
> You can't have him.
> Bring him back...

It's just stuff I told myself. Just stuff. I would not have used it, didn't need it. I was beginning to re-imagine my home, had wanted to clear space for new beginnings. These were guys who would make good use of his tools.

> But still my heart hurt.
> I felt like I sold him out.
> Gave him away for 30 pieces of silver.

Would it have made a difference if I'd donated those tools to Habitat for Humanity? Waited a little longer. Not sold them at all.

I took those dollar bills and treated my daughter to a lovely dinner. There was room in the garage now to relocate the washer and dryer so I could re-design my kitchen.

Still, that night I laid on the bed he built, placed my earrings in the jewelry case he made, and sobbed myself to sleep.

How do I make peace with that? I labeled myself Judas for looking to the future, for leaving him behind. Was I looking to forgive myself for nothing I'd done wrong?

I imagine Mike wouldn't want me to feel distraught. "It's only stuff, not me." He would say. "I will always be with you."

But in that moment, I confess I had no pat answer to the rending of my heart. Standing on the precipice looking forward while his shadow was left behind…

OUR HOUSE

S everal months after Mike died, I joined *Our House*, a support group where people gathered to talk about their losses, share their grief.

That first night I looked around the group, women and men from different walks of life, linked by this common denominator. The room was quiet, none of the typical chattering. We had all become members of a club no one wanted to join.

I wasn't sure if it would be a good fit for me. Would I be able to hold everyone's grief as well as my own. Would I find myself frustrated that I couldn't share all that I needed to? Would I start to weep and not be able to get a word out at all?

We took turns sharing our names, our spouse's name, and how they had died. Bringing ourselves and our loved ones into the circle. Tears rolled silently down cheeks, some rocked in their seats. As each one found the courage to reveal their story, I felt their pain along with my own.

In a society that has little patience for grief, and certainly not in public, there was something exquisite about this container. For 90 minutes, we allowed the masks to drop, we did not have to pretend or be strong. We sat as witnesses, with no fixing, no judgement. It was simply a place we could be ourselves in our grief.

The questions were implied: When would it end? When would we get better? When would the loneliness ease? When would we stop crying at the sight of their photos, the mention of their names?

The answers were not pat.

The journey would not be linear.

It was a spiral, a rollercoaster, a riptide, a river, a wave.

Wandering, weaving, reshaping, reforming, expanding, contracting.

With time and patience we would come through. Not necessarily to 'better,' but to different.

In our own time and in our own way.

As I put another foot forward on this path to 'different,' I found comfort in the gathering. Their stories were my stories, were our stories.

We were weaving a sacred circle to hold our tears and each other. As we made our way through the darkness of this tunnel, hands holding hands.

As we stumbled and fell,

Rose up and went on.

WITHOUT HIM

I t is strange the things that trigger the grieving. The other day it was a visit to the accountant.

Every year for 26 years we had our ritual at tax time. There was the argument over turbo tax vs. a professional. I always voted for the professional; I usually won. Then organizing the receipts. We'd take over the dining room table as we deciphered the little scraps of paper we'd accumulated throughout the year. Finally, we would take a weekend and sit side by side while he read the receipts out loud and I entered them into the computer.

I was the one who met with the accountant. After each appointment, I would sit in the car and call him to tell him the good / bad news. Then we would go out to celebrate we were done, at least for another year.

This year I was aware of his absence as I went through the process. No argument over the accountant, no one to help me sort the receipts. No one to sit by my side, coffee in hand, to read me the details. And no one to celebrate the refund we would be receiving this year…

Without him. That is my awareness now.

Everywhere I see his missingness, his absence. Like the crescent moon against a black sky, I am reminded how every little / big thing is now without him.

To bed I go without him.
To dinner I go without him.
To celebrate I do without him.
To shop or nap or dance or walk, I now do without him.

There is no one to scold, no one to hold.
No one to fight, no one to hug.
He is not there to squeeze me in his arms as I beat the floor with missing him.
Even this I must do without him.

There is no one to carry my bags,
Or tease me about my credit cards.
No one to dream with about travels, adventures, our future.
The list is endless; the big and little things I must now do without him.

But even as my heart clenches and my sobs rise, I also know this:
I have learned to go to bed without him.
To snuggle up against the pillow and the cat as I drift to sleep.
I carry my own bags without him,
Though sometimes it requires several trips to get them all inside.
I have talked to a plumber and climbed a ladder to change a lightbulb.
I have even fallen to the floor, and picked myself
up, repeatedly, all without him.
I am planning my travels, my adventures, my future …
Without him.

But I feel him!
I know he is here,
Whispering at my shoulder, slipping into dreams.
Encouraging me to be brave, to live big.
To travel the world and have my adventures.
To find joy and love and celebration.

I know, know, know,
That even as I move forward in this life without him,

He will always be a part of me.
He is woven into my heart,
Into my bones and sinews and muscles.

He has made me who I am.
He will always be my love.

Smoke and Coffee

I am curled in my sleeping bag. The tent has warmed up with two bodies in it. At some point I'll have to get up but for the moment I am content in my cozy nest. Outside I can hear him walking around, stoking the fire, the sounds of the birds and their wake-up call. The smell of smoke drifts in along with coffee, enticing me to rise.

It is indelibly imprinted in my memories, smoke and coffee.

He wears his camping hat, wool with a wide brim. Carries his walking stick. All bundled up in a jacket, once red, now a faded pink. And his hiking boots, which still sit by my washing machine, an odd testament to our life together.

He reaches into the tent, coffee in hand, perfectly prepared the way I like it, with cream and sugar. "The lark is up to greet the sun. Are you ready to rise?"

It's warm in my cocoon and yet I am ready to begin the day. "Yes," I say, taking the hot cup and sitting up to enjoy that first amazing sip. We joke that everything tastes better when we are camping.

I stretch out, bones creaking. Though I use two pads under my sleeping bag there is still this stiffness from lying on the hard ground. Holding the coffee precariously, one of those blue metal cups, it is still hot to touch. Then into pants and jacket, socks and shoes, and out I stumble. To make my way to the fire, now crackling merrily away.

This was our routine. He'd start the fire, make the coffee, and then after I'd had a cup or two, I would make breakfast.

I loved camping with him. Coffee and smoke. My clothes, my hair, infused with those smells. That's another thing about camping, you don't mind how you smell: smoke, sweat, feet.

One of the fun aspects of camping was discovering how necessity was truly the mother of invention. Interesting ways to prepare freeze dried eggs so they tasted better. The simple pleasure of washing hands and faces with water boiled over a camp stove. Roasted potatoes and onions buried in the coals. Once when we were backpacking, he made me a throne of tree logs to use as a bathroom since there were no toilets.

Then there was the quieting of my mind as it finally settled. I would read or write at the picnic table, and he'd go for his morning walkabout. The deep satisfaction of coming back from a long hike. Sitting and watching a crackling fire as the sky darkened. Fascinated as golden embers rose up to greet silver stars just peeking through.

Heading home, dry and dusty. The pleasure of thoroughly washing off the camping grime with the modern-day conveniences of hot showers, soap and shampoo. The relief of our soft bed, a warm kitchen, and the easy trip to the bathroom in the middle of the night.

Like a snapshot I hold it: That moment of him leaning into the tent, bringing with him the scent of the mountains, the trees, the smoke, the fresh brewed coffee. His smile.

I think this is when he was the happiest. Out in the mountains, smelling of coffee and smoke. Me with my hair wild and tangled, roasting marshmallows with our daughter, our little elf running around, her own wild self.

Sleeping when the day pulled our eyes shut. Voracious after a hike. Waking to the birdcalls and the stirring of the sleeping bag.

Just a little longer I say as I snuggle deeper. "Just a little longer."

THE CRACKED MIRROR

It was the first birthday without him. I turned 56. My daughter was moving to Colorado five days later. I looked in the mirror and felt old. Not just older, old.

It's not something we often admit, certainly not in public or polite company. And yet there it was. I looked in the mirror and saw ....

Skin that did not snap back the way it used to.

Wrinkles in new and ever-expanding places.

Gray hair that showed more quickly.

Age spots that had become constellations across my arms.

I needed glasses to put on my makeup.

Even the shape of my body was changing. No longer quite so pert nor quite so round.

Gravity was having her way with me.

I considered turning off the tap to this train of thought, but then decided, what the hell. In for a penny, in for a pound. Let it pour, let it rant, let it overflow the banks. No way out but through. And so, the pity party raged, and down the rabbit hole I tumbled.

Stories about being old and used up, with nothing to offer, and nothing to give. The flirting was finished, the feeling of being delicious and desirable, done. I imagined what it would be like to walk into a room and feel invisible, no longer noticed, or considered.

The painful questions seeped out from beneath mud and slime.

Who would want me now?

Who would want me like this?

Was this all that was left?

To wrinkle and dry, and ache and break, until one day I blew away like the dust we all return to.

Good Lord — take me.

At that point I considered gorging on pizza and Haagen Daz chocolate ice cream. But then I'd be sick as well as sad.

I sat with the spewing for a while, giving it permission to swirl and shift and finally settle. After a time, a voice asked, kindly, gently, "Is that what you truly believe?"

With a deep breath and a wiping of my eyes I considered and answered as truthfully as I could.

I acknowledged that this was a particularly challenging time, grieving and loss, and more change than I thought I could manage.

I acknowledged it hurt, still hurt, all hurt, though not as much as before.

I acknowledged I was getting older, closer to 100 than to 10.

But I also noticed how many of those fears were based on how I thought I would be perceived. Noticed many of the fears were based on an 'outside' looking in.

And those fears were fed voraciously by a culture that wanted us to believe we were not enough, never enough.

Instead, we were taught to consume, and yearn, and follow the leader like good little sheep, in hopes that one day we would find our way to enough.

But we had been given a cracked mirror.

So, what could I learn from this raging pity party?

It was good to let it out.

It was good to purge it.

It was good to shake it, bake it, burn it out.

And then it was time to put that cracked mirror down.

It was time to see with eyes of love and compassion, kindness and trust. To believe there was meaning to it all, even if we didn't know what. To trust we had been gifted with this life, this mystery, and that it was ours to experience until our very last breath.

I couldn't change that I would age. At some point, my body would give out and I would die, a fact, like taxes. I confess it frightened me.

But until then, I could choose how I lived my life. I could choose to write and perform and create until the day I couldn't lift my pen or speak a word. I could choose to travel the world and learn to sail a boat or fly a plane (maybe not the plane). I could choose to enter a room and reach out to friends and strangers, believing I was seen, welcomed.

We all get to choose. In this great mystery and wonder, we have been given the gift of life. It is for us to take the days, months, moments we have been granted and live, be they good days or bad. It is for us to live as fully, as thoroughly, as richly, as we desire.

PARALLEL UNIVERSE

The layers, the textures of grief shift and change, deepen. The shock wears off and we are faced with a new reality.

I've heard it described as 'surreal,' this life after death. This existence that no longer resembles past experiences, though it feels like it should. In this inexplicable parallel universe, I can see that other life out of the corner of my eye. Catching glimpses of it when I'm not looking.

Mike sitting in his chair doing his crossword puzzles while I write my morning pages on the couch. Our evening walks, arm in arm, to the grocery store where he would buy an ice cream sandwich and I would take nibbles as we walked home. His ritual of recording five or six soccer games to watch over the weekend.

But when I look again, the chair is empty, the television silent, and I don't walk to the grocery store in the evenings anymore.

Is it better to remember or less painful to forget....

There are days, still, when I literally don't know how to breathe. Great big gasping breaths that can't seem to fill my lungs. But there are also moments when I laugh, deep belly laughs I'd forgotten I could.

Several days in a row when I don't cry at all, though I more than make up for it afterwards. Conversations that no longer begin with "I lost my husband a few days / weeks / months... ago."

I see it, feel it, the river that flows on, endlessly, as the rest of the world races forward. The temptation is to give in.

> Get pulled along with the current.
> Get back to 'normal.'
> Get busy.
> Get doing.
> Get on with it, already.

The voice that whispers I'm lazy, indulgent, self-involved. How much longer? Life goes on.

But then I remember what I felt as I saw his body lying on the table, his spark of life gone. What an ephemeral miraculous gift we've been given.

And how exquisitely tenuous it all is.

I let that harsh voice roll over me, choosing otherwise. Trusting that for me this is a time for going under, sinking beneath the waves. Curling up in the comfort of the dark soil to let the healing continue. Letting the journey take me inwards rather than out.

Trusting that when the time is ripe, I will know it. Emerging from winter into spring all in good time.

Coroner Report

I t took eight months to find the courage to order the coroner's report. It was hard enough taking each step forward without having to be dragged back to those first horrific days.

With a bit more distance, I thought it was time, not just for me, but for the rest of his family, to try to understand the truth of what happened on that operating table.

Fourteen pages of body parts and words I couldn't pronounce, much less understand. Hard to look at the report and imagine this was my husband, had been my husband. The memories that tumbled in nearly crushed me:

They'd kept him at the hospital for several days before they released him to the coroner's office.

They'd kept him in the morgue for weeks because they were backlogged with other more urgent cases.

His body lay cold and alone while we waited for him to be released back to us.

I didn't want to consider what it meant, what they needed to do, to conduct that autopsy.

My sweet husband had become bones and organs and body parts, measured and weighed and dissected as they sought to reveal what happened.

The great mystery of what animates us will not be found in bones and blood and tissue. I felt its missingness the afternoon I said goodbye. His body looked the same, and yet he didn't. His skin cool to the touch, his lips already turning blue. His eyes closed. I touched his face, his hair, kissed his cheek, and said goodbye.

As I raised myself from his body I understood in a deeper way that our lives were a miracle. It was an ephemeral thing that separated life from death. The light, spirit, soul that animated his body had moved on, no longer there in his smile, his touch, his laugh.

But his memory, our love, that would live on.

DARK QUEENS

I've started gorging on food,
To full and beyond.
Eat and stuff, eat and stuff.
Chicken and bread and cheese and peanut butter.

Seeking to fill the void.
But not just the void, the Other.

Going back to the refrigerator again and again,
Devouring seconds and thirds.
Shoveling mouthfuls of rice while I stand at the sink.
It hurts and still I eat.

It is not loneliness that hungers. It is not even grief.
I have grown oddly comfortable with grief.
I know what it feels like to sink to my knees and sob.
To give in to the flood of tears.

But this feeding of the void is something else.
What flesh and blood and muscle and sinew must I give
To appease this hunger?

It lurks in the shadows, this.
In the deep dark shadows, this.
No candle burns here, no sweet light.
This is not for white lace hankies and delicate tears.
You are chained in the darkness,
Buried beneath the grief.

Hunger, you are here.

My Dark Queens, you are here.

Anguish. Fury. Rage. Impotence. Guilt.
What do you need to be set free?
How do I howl you free?

Feed us. They cry.
See us. They beg.
Bring us into the light! They roar.

In the safety of the circle, I surrender.
Open the doors to the dark dungeon.
Let them rise up in me.

Bent back, twisted legs, hooked fingers, gargoyle faces.
Grunts and howls and moans as my Queens blaze up,
Roaring through me, a wildfire.

At the injustice.
At the surgeon who should have known better.
At the I'm sorry's that don't bring him back.
At the years ripped from us.

Eventually the music slows, my body stills.
The Dark Queens ease back into the shadows.
They are quiet now, at peace,
For a while at least.
The cravings have eased,
For a while at least.

In the last lingering notes of the song, I hear…
Do not forget us.

LETTER FROM MY GRIEF

Grief, write me a letter,
Telling me it's ok
To feel what I feel,
Think what I think.

She answered:

Let it be, Love. Let it be.
There is nothing to prove, no timeline to meet.
It is a road you walk alone, but it need not be lonely.
Humankind walks this road, whether we acknowledge it or not.

The wolf howls to a sky of endless stars. Singing
its desire to join, commune, belong.

We are friends here, comrades in arms.
The well fills and fills and overflows.
I am the mirror to your love.
The reminder of your great big heart.

It is an honor to feel me.
To know you have loved,
To know you can feel,
To know you are human.

To be the conduit, the permission for others

To drink from my cup and not be afraid.

Why are you so afraid of me?
Dark side of the moon.
Afraid if you let me in, you will drown in your
sorrow, never feel the light again.

Sink into my arms, beloved.
Find comfort in the sorrow,
In the longing, in the yearning.

I am the shadow.
I am the Shiva to the Shakti.
I am the space to the form.
I am the black night to the endless stars.
I am the reflection of your love.

I ask: "How do I dance with you, Grief?"

As you have, by writing.
Honor me with your movement,
With your stillness.

The rituals are there for the making.
Together we will make them, sing them, write them, dance them.
You and him and me, together we will dance.

I may rise huge, tidal wave huge.
But you will not drown,
I promise you, you will not drown.

You / we will ride that wave. Surfer girls.
Ha, there it is, playful. We are surfer girls riding the waves of grief.
Turn on the Beach Boys and ride my back.

I ask: "Do I want you gone?"

I am here for the transition,
I am part of the transformation,
Part of the alchemy to help you heal.

I am mystery and mystic and magic.
There is such power to feeling me completely.
To know you can ride the wave and survive.

One day I will no longer be so necessary.
Like a mother I will let you go.
Though you know we will meet again.

But there is no timeline, we need no proof.
We stand waiting, for when you/me are ready.

Do not apologize for me,
Do not make me small,
Do not pretend I do not exist.

Let me breathe,
Let me flow.
Into my arms, let yourself fall.

FAITH

Do not lose faith. Do not lose hope.

When we are in the depths of it, unable to see past the pain
that rips us apart, we cannot believe that anything else is
possible. That we will ever smile, laugh, celebrate, love again.

But I am here, years later, to tell you, yes, it is possible. Though this
journey through the dark lands is uniquely yours, you can find your way.

And as much as I wish it, there is no magic spell, no shortcut. We
must be patient. But it does change. In its own time, in its own way.

The grip loosens a little bit, the dark lightens.

One day you will be surprised that loss is not the first thing you think
of when you awaken. It is not your last thought as you close your eyes.

One day you are amazed to discover that you can imagine a future beyond.

ENERGY OF THINGS

I looked around my house trying to decide what to do with Mikes things. We'd been married for twenty-six years. We'd raised a family, built a home. His death had been unexpected, with no time to prepare.

"There is no rush, take your time. Things have energy and you will know when it is time." This was the wisdom of Ziri Rideaux, the fabulous owner of *Friends Funeral Home*, who helped guide me through the process.

As my daughter and I sat there trying to absorb our new reality, Ziri reminded us that everything was energy, and that over time energy changes. There was no need to rush to do anything. When the time was right decisions would become clear. I took that to heart, trusting the impulses as they rose, noting my reactions to things, both his and mine.

In some cases, it was almost violent. "Throw it away. NOW!" We had an old comforter that was losing its feathers, ink stains in the corner. I'd wanted to get rid of it for ages, but for whatever reason he didn't want to let it go.

Each morning after he died, I'd get up and make the bed, hating that damn comforter. It bothered me until one afternoon I dragged my mom off to Macy's and we found a beautiful quilt to replace it. Something eased when I spread that quilt out for the first time, with its white and blue flowers.

Then there were those crazy things, items I knew I would throw away, but just couldn't touch yet.

Before he went into the hospital Mike had been building a trellis. He'd put everything away except for a pair of gloves he'd left on the back steps, a ratty old pair, ripped and falling apart.

For weeks I left those gloves on the stoop, as though at any moment he would return to pick them up and get back to work. I told my daughter not to touch them. Carefully, I'd sit on the steps so as not to disturb them. Sometimes both of us would squeeze onto the steps, drinking our morning coffee, and still, I would not move them.

Then one morning, we began cleaning the garage and I walked past those gloves; something had changed. The energy of them had shifted. For the last time I looked at them before picking them up and throwing them away.

Then, of course, there were the landmines. Untouchable, unthinkable.

His closet was in my office, the door firmly closed. A laundry basket of his clothes had been tossed inside; the door slammed shut before I could look further. It wasn't until the family came together for the memorial months later that we opened the door and went through his items.

Each piece had its memories, textures, smells. The suits he wore to work. The Hawaiian shirts he wore to parties. His favorite t-shirts, so beloved there were holes worn into the fabric. One by one, around and around, we decided. Keep. Donate. Throw away.

Slowly, at my own pace, I went through the house, resolving to keep only what was beautiful, what pleased me. Over time, I got braver, claiming the house as my own in bigger ways. Painting the bedroom, re-doing the garden, upgrading the bathroom.

How much harder it must be when we are forced to immediately empty out a space. Like amputating a leg or arm, as we are pushed to decide what to keep, discard or donate without the time to release it in our hearts first.

I am grateful I had the option to adjust slowly, to let my insides shift to accommodate the changing energy of his things. It is a never-ending lesson in listening and trusting that when the time is right, we will know it.

TASTING WILD

W ild. Wild is any place far from here. I feel so far from wild. Everything is tamped down, closed in tight. The dam sits just beyond with nothing but a tiny hole between me and utter chaos.

If I could, I would stand at the edge of the deepest canyon, on the peaks of mountains high. If I could, I'd watch the storm come roaring in and dance with the tempest it brought.

Wild would be standing in a rain forest feeling the drops falling, washing me clean. Launching myself from the tallest tree to surf the currents of the wind. Wild would be shrieking at the top of my lungs, laughing loudly, beating my chest. My body pounding to the drums, dripping with sweat and exhaustion, fully danced out.

Wild is unkempt, unfettered, untamed. Stepping where I want without worrying about toes, or who's feelings might be hurt.

Wild is senses fully alive, touch, taste, smell, especially smell. To breath in earth, green, sea, desert, lust. It ripples into my brain and through my body. I am it. I am sea, forest, soil.

Wild is becoming, it is feeling it all. Intense, not diluted. Not halfway or just short of the truth.

I can taste wild on my tongue, just out of reach. It is painful to long for it and not be able to reach it.

Once upon a time, wild was calling out to my lover and begging him to take me harder, rippling with desire and release that sent me soaring to the sun.

Wild was taking a breath and tapping into Source. Holy shit, what was that?

Wild was childbirth, when I was caught and carried by the river, lost my paddles and could do nothing but trust I would come safely to shore.

Wild was faith. Wild was trust.

Wild is nothing I feel these days. Wild is simply wanting to escape this cage.

I am desperate for wild. Behind my glass prison everything feels muted and numb. I pound at the door of freedom, pray for a breath of air, but nothing answers except, "Go another day, take another step."

But wild isn't always big leaps and loud noises. Sometimes wild is simply speaking the truth.

Wild is not sugarcoating this road I'm on. Wild is not being anything other than what I feel.

Wild was, and still is, trust, faith. Stepping into the void, the unknown, knowing I will be held, I will be caught.

Wild is deep breath after deep breath. I need an infinite amount of breath. Cleansing, pure, sweet.

Wild is the silver bell pealing at dawn.

You are alive.

You are alive.

WISDOM OF A SIX-YEAR-OLD

R elax. Breathe. Focus. Those were the words my friend whispered as I precariously made my way across a slack line for the first time.

He whispered them a second time as I gripped his hand a little less tightly. And again, a third, as I risked letting him go for a split second before lunging for the pole at the end of the line.

I jokingly said it sounded like a metaphor for life. He nodded his head.

It had been a hard few weeks. Spring used to be our favorite season with its slew of celebrations: my birthday, his birthday, our anniversary, Mother's Day, Father's Day. Now, I rode out each of those days with his loss reverberating in my heart, an anvil striking.

One day I went searching through his jacket pockets with the odd hope of finding some remembrance of him I'd missed. Some little sign he was still around, that this was just a bad dream. All I found was a crumpled piece of tissue and a couple of paper clips.

It hadn't occurred to me, but it seemed the colors of the grief kept changing, the nuances to the loss, the heartache. This season the color of grief was loneliness. In the beginning, I welcomed being alone. I needed the privacy and space to let it roar through me without having to put on a happy face and pretend like things were ok.

But as I sobbed in the shower and wept by the sea, I felt how alone in all this of I was. My mind went to town on the fears. What would happen if I got sick? Who would be there for me when I got old? Who would love me no matter what? I went through my little black book of family and friends and ruled them out one by one. Each person had their own life to live, their own burdens to carry. I didn't want to bother them with how, after nearly a year, it still hurt so much.

So, I sat with alone and loneliness and sorrow.

Then something odd happened. The little girl who used to sit on the bench at recess because she was so shy took a deep breath, stood up, and boldly said, "I want to play. I want to be with people. I don't want to sit here alone anymore and just watch."

It was such a strong impulse I couldn't refuse. So, on a beautiful warm afternoon, I made my way down to the beach where friends gathered to work out with rings, hula hoops, and slack lines. It was intimidating, all those strong athletic bodies moving so gracefully and powerfully. That was not me by long shot. I almost changed my mind. Almost.

But my little girl wanted to play, needed to play. It had been such a long time. I took a deep breath, let go of embarrassment and asked, "Can you show me? Will you teach me?"

Wheeeee! Wheeeee! Wheeeee! Jumping up and down with fun and laughter. How to express the incredible joy of that afternoon. Feeling like I belonged, no longer sitting on the sidelines looking on. Instead, I was simply having the experience, with no judgement, no fear. Even if I worried I'd fall or look silly, none of that mattered. It was just play.

My body hummed with pleasure. She delighted in the sense of accomplishment as she tried out new skills. True, she shook and fell and missed. But she also succeeded! She walked the line, caught the ring, hulaed the hoop. It was delicious to feel the ache in her quads, the tightness in her muscles, at these new-found activities.

I'd forgotten my adventurous six-year-old used to walk fearlessly along a 4" wide railing at the playground. She tied a sheet to the stairwell and swung down the steps. Piled pillows at the base of the refrigerator and dropped off the side. All for the thrill of it.

She was still here.

I walked home that evening in the cooling air, a bounce in my step, re-living the sensations of the afternoon. I knew there were dark days ahead. I was not done with tears and longing and loneliness. The waves would no doubt raise me up and drag me under.

But in all of that, I also knew there was pleasure to be found, joy to be discovered.

Sometimes, our six-year-old knows best.

Listening to the Quiet

Thanksgiving, and I hit the landmine that was the 'holidays.' My daughter and I had been invited back east to join his family. I didn't know if I had it in me to go. That time of year was particularly charged, laden with rituals and traditions, glaring with his missingness.

We decided yes and made the pilgrimage east to be with them. Five hours flying, then five hours driving, as we made our way up into the beauty of the Adirondacks.

It was ironic that this gathering was meant to have been a family reunion. We hadn't all been together, descendants of mother, Betty and father, Chaunce, in over seven years. Just the year before, Mike and I had gone to Maine to visit his cousin. It was there we decided to gather the family for the following Thanksgiving.

He would have loved this weekend. I could imagine him there. Relishing his clan, eating too much, challenging his cousins to chess. Running out with them to play soccer in the snow, then curling up with a book by the fire, giving me his "I'm so very happy we are here," grin.

Many of his family had not been able to make it to the memorial, so it felt good to come together to share. Bittersweet that we were gathered at the table, and he was not there. Though oddly, we miscounted the number of place settings and ended up with one extra setting, right next to me. So, who is to say...

Over the weekend, we created a board with photos of him at all ages. One night I stood in front of it with colored pens, inspired to weave my words with images of his face. In the magic of that moment, these words flowed from my fingers:

Time travelers to worlds unknown, waiting
for us patiently on the other side.
You must laugh at what awaits us. Words not found for places not seen.

Then I heard his voice,
"Surprise, surprise." He chuckled.

My camper man, my motorcycle man.
Always he had bright eyes filled with such wonder.
Deep warm heart opening and unfolding.
There, always there. My rock, my roots, my love.
Woven into my heart and strands of thought.
His spirit, his soul, at my shoulder like a guide.

"Be not afraid." He whispered.
"We are infinite. There are such wonders beyond.
But this life as you know it, is finite.
This time, it is precious, precious time.
So Live. Live. Live. Live.
Rise to meet the sun.
Kiss the moon.
Leap with the waves.
Live life. Love life.

Find wonder and laughter and joy.
Listen and explore.
Adventure, it is all such an adventure.
From the single snowflake to the mountain high.
From your first love to your final breath.
It is all such an adventure.

> Listen to your heart,
> To the wind,
> To the sand blowing across the dunes.
> To the laughter and the sparkle.
> And to the quiet. Most importantly,
> Listen to the quiet..."

And then it was still.

On the last day we crunched through fresh fallen snow to sprinkle his ashes at the base of a twin-trunked poplar. We gathered in a circle holding hands. Listened to a poem written in his honor and sang the chorus to "What the World Needs Now." In spring they would plant a tree.

Then, one by one, the gathering disbursed as family members headed home. Finally, it was our turn to pack up the car and share one last round of goodbyes.

The thing that struck me most profoundly was that somehow his missingness had woven us more tightly together. In the truth of this time, as we hugged and cried and missed him and others who were gone, we opened and softened and revealed.

In grieving together, we embraced and held each other, belonging in a way we had not before.

THE WATERS

The holidays were officially over. I would never have to live through another first Christmas after his death. Did that mean it got easier?

Sometimes.

Sometimes there were days when the waters were flat, the seas calm. I could see a horizon in the distance, faint, far away, but visible none-the-less.

Sometimes the fog crept in. The chill danced down my neck, my back, my legs and I shivered. I looked around but the way was hidden, and I seemed to drift endlessly. I prayed for a break in the clouds, a ray of light to show the way. But the gray grew darker, seeping further into my heart, until all I wanted was to sink below the waters and sleep.

And sometimes it was impossible to avoid monsoon season, with hurricanes and tidal waves that smashed me to the ground.

During those times, all I could do was fall to my knees as my head, my heart, my tears sought the floor for safety.

It was not possible to stand at all. There were no thoughts of the horizon, the future, distant places.

Only survival.

Breathe.

Sometimes we just need to remember to breathe.

EMERGING

It is one step forward, two steps
back, three steps sideways.

Like a crab, a snake, a beetle.

One step, stop. Stumble, fall, get up.

Begin again.

I spent a long time emerging.

No set boundary, no clearly defined lines.

ACCLIMATING

O n May 8 I hit the one-year anniversary of Mike's death. For weeks I'd been preparing for it, gearing up for another sharp bolt of pain. I gave myself lots of space to grieve, my heart listening for any clues as to how I would ride this tidal wave of my first year as widow.

And then it was May 9.

And nothing changed.

Somewhere along the line, I heard, or wanted to believe, that after the first year things would start to get better. Even though other widows spoke of three and four years before they started to feel 'normal' again, I hoped I would get to that point sooner. And when that didn't happen, when I still felt heart-broken, untethered, lost, the swamp monsters slithered out in force, sharp tongued and cruel.

"It's been a year already. You need to get back out into the world. It's time to get on with it. Look at everyone who has it so much worse than you. Stop feeling sorry for yourself. Folks are tired of you being so sad all the time."

I dropped into the abyss, tumbling past compassion, kindness, patience, gentleness, love. Falling beyond the loving hands of family, friends, support. I could feel it happening and could do nothing to prevent it.

In that place of gray I felt completely abandoned. All those loved ones were simply phantoms, their words of support and encouragement sliding past like mist. I nodded my head but heard nothing. Most painfully, I felt abandoned by myself. The soul, the 'me,' I had felt through even the most anguished moments was no longer accessible. I had nothing left, or so I believed.

Sitting in the therapist's office, I tried to explain this deep aloneness, the untethered, off-centeredness I felt. She listened, then suggested a different perspective.

What if this gray place was the space I needed to learn new steps to the dance.

In the beginning steps are wobbly and unsure, the floor uneven, the music unrecognizable. The partner is unknown, and we cannot find our balance. But in time, with practice and patience, we become more confident, requiring less thought. In time, we can feel into the music, trust our partner will catch us, find pleasure in the dance. Our hands swing a little further, our legs lift a little higher. We don't have to think about it so much, we can just enjoy.

As the first year flowed into the second, I realized in yet another way, my life had radically changed. My husband of 26 years was no longer with me in the physical realm. And though I'd made the one year mark some arbitrary line in the sand, loaded with expectations and projections, the process was what it was. No rushing, no pushing, no forcing.

Easier said than done, to ignore the desperate hope that it would end, the pain, the depression, the life half-lived. How could I accept where I was and let it unfold in its own way? How could I ride the grief, accept the gray, rejoice in the spots of greens and oranges when they did arrive? How could I continue to heal with kindness and self-care, letting go of judgement and resentment that I wasn't doing it right or fast enough? Letting go of the desire to be able to get on with my life.

When this *was* my life.

> Every breath, every tear
> Every moment of hearing the birds sing in the morning
> Sitting in the garden with my cat
> Dancing with the waves
> Sleeping
> Reading
> Eating
> Dishes, laundry, wiping down the kitchen sink

Taking out the trash
Culling the weeds
Doing nothing important
Doing nothing

I searched for a word that could capture this time. The word was not "waiting," for that implied the anticipation of something better, of wanting to be elsewhere. No, the word that came to mind was *acclimating*.

I was acclimating to this new life. Like a deep-sea diver or a mountain climber who had to pause as their bodies adjusted to changes in altitude.

It would be a time, for as long as it took, for my body and mind to adjust and accept the new altitude, the new reality. It seemed that during that time I needed to sleep more, read more, do little, more. It was a time to let go of accomplishments, goals, plans, tomorrow.

Acclimate also implied I would continue. There was a future that awaited. But there was also sweet permission to be still, to let molecules realign in their own time, with no expectation, no rush.

ROOM TO BREATHE

You halt, stop at the door.
Looking left, right. Hesitating.
What / you wait.
What / you want.

You find your own Morse code of writing.
Step out. Step through. To the other side.
Where you breathe, rich and deep.
You breathe, rich and deep.

There is room.

Between the lines, between the words.
Breathe.

Your own words, what are your own words?
They are your words, my words, our words.
Yes, space between lines, between words.

A poem of space between words and lines and thoughts.

Space for thoughts to ebb and flow. To dance
Without stepping on toes.
To waltz to a music soft and sweet. Space for us to breathe and allow.
In the silence, in the space, to allow.

Birthing, whispering, baby steps and twirls.
To come through with room to expand.
A bubble fills but does not burst.
A wide field, a mountain top, an ocean magnificent and blue.

A breath so deep, so true.

You inhale the world, then set Spirit free.
She kisses our insides, blesses us with her touch.
Inside and outside, she dances, weaving us whole.
Shuttling in and out, weaving us whole.

Space and room to breathe and dance.
To try /to explore
To begin / to end
To touch / to taste
To consider / to contemplate
To expand / to grow
To touch the edges of infinity with room for more.

What do you need? Room to breathe and space to move.
This dance is ours, yours and mine.

How do we find each other when you doubt, or I fear.
Crowding, hiding, disappearing into small and tiny.

Breathe and find this place, this space, where there is room for us.
For you to find me.

Here there is room to splash paints and leap on walls.
To pluck music from the air because it pleases us.
Here is the land of magic and mystery.

Begin here, from the center of the spiral, begin from the center of it all.
Breathe in. Breathe out.
Touch the edges of infinity and beyond.

Where there is room to breathe and space to dance.

ALASKA

T he name rose up like a word of power, a word of promise.

I had been writing about it. How it had become a place I still wanted to visit but would no longer do so with my husband. And if I went, I would not camp as we'd originally planned, but rather join a cruise, with its safe comfortable way of viewing the wilderness.

But then later that day, out of the blue, my brave, world traveling daughter asked if I'd be interested in going with her to Alaska for the June 24 summer solstice. A friend of hers was from Anchorage and had encouraged her to visit. His family owned a bush plane company, and he would be happy to help plan the trip.

Pristine, wild, home of the Aurora Borealis. It had called my name, a siren song to my heart, for years. I remember the first time I considered visiting. Mike and I had gone to a travel convention, stopping at various booths to learn about Spain, Utah, Costa Rica.

As we walked down one of the halls, I looked up and spotted a giant poster of Mt. Denali looming huge and majestic, wild and beckoning among the clouds. I felt a ripple move through me, as the vision tugged. I grabbed Mike's arm and pointed, "Yes, yes! That is a place we must go."

To my daughter I said, "Yes. Yes. I will go with you."

Like other choices I'd made over the past months, this road to Alaska unrolled before me, as if it was already done.

June 24. The summer solstice. The longest day of the year. I imagined breathing deep of that clear crisp air. A chill running through me as I looked up into a dark black sky with its million brilliant stars. I would feel alive there.

Alaska, with its wonders to explore, its majesty to bow before. It was a place to be reborn.

If We Build It -
Planting a
Healing Garden

I had been anticipating this planting day for weeks. Journaling about it, sketching ideas, taking trips to the nursery for inspiration. The day dawned beautiful, bright but not too hot. Late fall was a perfect time for planting in Southern California.

My landscaper had come the day before to do some of the heavier work, installing decomposed granite between the pavers, putting lights up in the trees, planting the larger specimens. But I had always imagined the planting of the garden would be my work.

Thanks to my daughter, several of her friends showed up to help. They were young, strong, and happily willing. "What do you need? Tell us what to do?" For the next few hours, we dug and watered and eased plants into the ground.

"Gently, gently." I reminded them. We started in the backyard, moved into the front. Neighbors came up, curious to see what we were up to, excited to view the finished product.

Repeatedly I thanked these young folks for coming to help. Over and over, they told me they'd enjoyed it. For several, it took them back to their childhoods when there had been family gardens to tend. My daughter admitted that she hadn't touched our garden since she was six years old.

At the end of the day, we sat on the porch, our planting party pooped. As I looked around at these beautiful beings, tired, with smudges on their faces, talking and laughing, I became aware of something. Throughout the experience, I had assumed that their participation had been a favor to us after losing Mike. However, in doing that, I underestimated them and forgot some very important lessons.

I confused favor with gifting. In my mind, these young people could easily have spent their Saturday in some other way, much more fun. But to them, this day was their gift, to my daughter, to me. They found genuine pleasure in the giving of their time and energy to create something beautiful that would bring joy and healing.

I also saw that working in the garden was a gift to them. We all yearn for that connection to the earth, young or old, all colors of the rainbow, all systems of belief, all economic strata. This favor was an opportunity for them to come together as friends, to put their hands in the soil, and to care for living things. This day was a chance to experience a primal connection to the earth.

So, I gladly accepted their great kindness. There was a deep satisfaction in the community we shared, using our hands, our strength, to build this garden. There was also the knowledge that when they visited in the future, they would appreciate the space differently, as they literally helped make it what it was.

On that day I was reminded of the infinite possibilities that are always present as the road shifts and forks and shifts again. Even as the losses tear us asunder, there are new experiences to be had, new gifts to be received.

BRAVERY IS RELATIVE

Quivering, shivering, hummingbird heart.
Shoulders tight, breath quick,
Belly clenching and wrenching.

This was no leaping from a plane, no diving from a cliff. This was simply my dread at the thought of returning home from Corvallis, Oregon.

The trip had been intended as my first solo flight. Portland seemed like a safe choice. It was a beautiful city with great public transportation, easy to get to. And best of all, I had three friends who now made their home there.

I registered with Air BnB, delighted at the cozy room I found, bought my tickets, and rented a car. This was good, I knew how to do this. There was a tremor of anticipation at this undertaking, the potential for pleasure in discovering a new place. And under it all, I needed to prove to myself I could do this.

But as to be expected, the experience was mixed. Memories stirred as I remembered how much fun Mike and I had travelling together. The adventure of figuring out transportation, the joy of discovering some hidden corner, the pleasure of hikes in the woods, and bedtime curled up cozy.

Numerous times I wanted to snap a picture and send it to him, "Hey honey, look at this, a wishing tree, a great café, my cool room…" In my mind I saw his reaction as he'd text me back with his day's activities.

Yet woven into the sadness was also the acknowledgement that bit by bit I was relearning how to walk, finding the courage to venture out to places unknown. I was beyond grateful to join dear friends for a delicious dinner, flowing with love, tears, compassion, and promise.

Doing good, I thought to myself as I made my way down to Corvallis where my third friend lived.

> In the pouring rain,
> In a car not mine,
> On a road not known.
> Doing good.

But when it was time to head home, my courage deserted me. I had given myself seven hours to get from Corvallis to the airport in Portland, 90 miles away. My logical mind said that was plenty of time. But it wasn't my logical mind that came out to play.

Somehow, slippery snakes of fear were wrapping their cold skin around my heart, my stomach, my throat and the panic was rising. My imagination ran rampant.

> At thoughts of driving in a thunderstorm,
> Finding no gas,
> Being late to return the car,
> Getting lost on the way to the bus station,
> My flight getting delayed.

All I wanted was to be home. Safe.

I stood there in her kitchen, staring at my friend, deer in the headlights. "I don't know if I can do this." I whispered.

And this dear friend, who'd lost a loved one as well that year, told me she understood. She understood how hard it could be to take the smallest of steps, how overwhelming even the simplest of things could seem. But she would help me however she could, cheering me on all the way home.

Somehow, I made it back. Her texts were the guideposts.

> Arrived in Portland – Yeah!
> Got to the bus station – Hurrah!
> At last, at the airport – Good for you!

HOME! HOME! – Be well, sleep tight!

Years ago, my father looked at me the same way, terrified at simple tasks. My mother did as well, as she was lost in her dementia. And I understood. I understood in a way I had not before.

How terrifying simple things could feel. How quickly the panic rose to overwhelm us. How in a split second everything that felt solid collapsed at our feet.

This experience reminded me that we must be kind with ourselves and with others. We need to be gentle with our souls, loving, patient and compassionate. We don't know what it is to walk in another's shoes.

When we have lost our footing, and the forest is dark, sometimes the smallest steps require the greatest courage. Bravery is all relative.

SURRENDER

S oft animal burrowing, hiding her head beneath blankets. Escaping into a sleep so deep the dreams can't follow. Cringing at the thought of a new day.

This morning there is nothing to look forward to, nothing to pull me into the sun. I am on automatic pilot, with work, even with my writing. I am going through the motions. Sometimes that is what is necessary to get us through, going through the motions.

This is not a cheer me up writing, just what is true, right now. This is what I am feeling, or not feeling, after morning pages, a movement practice, a third cup of coffee. And still nothing lifts the gray.

I try to hold onto it's not always like this. There are other days, sparkle days, lift into the sky days, the world is my oyster days. Days when it is a joyous day and I want to breathe it all in. But today isn't one of those days.

Today the lift barely gets me off the ground. Today I want to burrow in the soil and hold my grief like a tender baby. Today I am sad and hurt and lonely, missing mother and lover and self. Today I feel like a paddle boat in the middle of the Pacific, where the waves are big and the skies dark, and there is such a sense of alone.

So, surrender. Don't go looking for the feel better solutions, the happy pill. Surrender to the anxiety, the sadness, the edge to this existence. Surrender when the tricks don't work, and the friends have nothing left to say, and numbness is found in television and chocolate ice cream.

Surrender to the missing, to the loneliness, to the emptiness. Surrender to the "What's the point?" I find myself counting down the days and counting down the nights, but to what end?

So today give in to sadness, feed it like an offering to the gods. Today it is ok to go through the motions, to not get straight A's, or ring the bright bell.

But these unhappy days are not wasted days. They are another moment in the dance. Going in and out, finding comfort when and where we can. Riding that paddle boat under dark gray skies.

Going through the motions and letting it be ok. Letting go of judgement when I am not bright yellow and orange. Reminding myself I moved, I wrote. I'll teach tonight, and I'll work. And I'll breathe and walk and smell and eat and sleep.

It is not a wasted day. I have paid attention to my heart. I have written on the page. In a while I'll step outside and breathe in the sweet scent of trees after rain. At some point, the gray clouds will lighten and shift. They always do.

In every day there is a lesson, a learning, a knowing. Don't rush, don't push. Allow it to move through you. A rainstorm heading east, followed by a new dawn.

So, surrender to this day, to going through the motions. Surrender to sadness and loneliness and patience and time.

Fast is not the winner.

Finished is not the goal.

Take your time,
Let it flow.
Surrender.

LETTER TO MY ARTIST, IN SOFT DEVOTION

Hello, you. I've missed you. It seems I've turned you away. Placed you in front of the television, set you up with a book, or even put you down for an early nap. All so I could have time to work. I almost wrote 'real work,' but caught myself. That is not true.

You have been patient, but you are tired of being ignored, forgotten. Passed over for the sake of spreadsheets and reports. You don't give a rat's ass about spreadsheets and reports.

You want to tell stories, go on adventures, try on someone else's skin so you can feel it all. I promised to never abandon you again. And yet.

I can feel my missing you. The growing discomfort every time I choose work over you. Ignoring the impulse, turning away your plea.

Yes, I put you in the backseat for a little while, but I didn't forget. I could see you in the rearview mirror. I begged you for patience, a little more time.

You are here, in my heart, in my pulse. I search for windows, pockets of time, when I can bring you out to play, to dance.

I hear your voice, "Don't just tell me you love me, miss me. Show me. Prove it to me. Make time for me."

It is October and the smell of heat and fall mingle. I want to be outside breathing it in deeper.

I make my promise to show up here with you, even if it is the crack of a window. Even if that window is only 5 minutes long. Maybe the crack isn't all about writing but allowing for woolgathering or looking at photographs. I consider how much bigger my window could get if I cut out social media and the news. Goodness, how much fresher the air, how much clearer the space, if I didn't let all that poison my time.

There is permission and kindness in being with you. I don't need a harsh task master or the sting of guilt to come to you. I come to you in love and joy, and because being with you is when I feel alive and whole and deeply satisfied.

I will hold cracks in the windows and pockets of time open for you. I promise, as long as there is paper and pen, no one will take that from me.

PERMISSION

I feel like the dark side of the moon. I am always myself, but these past weeks have been quiet, slumbering, not yet ready to dance with the sun. Not yet ready to step out of the shadows, to shout out with joy. Here I am. This is who I am. This is how I want to express myself.

I give myself permission to express quietly, with slow steps and a veil of gray. Permission to whisper words with no need to prove anything or convince anyone.

This dance is for me alone.

Permission to sit and sleep and ponder and wait. Permission to whine and complain. Permission to ask big questions and not worry about having the answers. Permission to answer to no one and nothing. But to lean into a chuckle or a smile and see where it takes me.

Permission to be fascinated by mundane things. The cat cleaning his whiskers, the hummingbird darting in for a drink of nectar. Permission to not come up with a third example even though the writer in me thinks there should be.

Permission to be unmotivated. To wait in stillness. Permission to write for myself and no one else. To let go of the need for approval or acceptance. Permission to exist wholly in and of myself.

Even these words feel false and forced and that is ok, too. I am on wobbly legs and that is ok.

So, more permission. For no expectations, no assumptions, no judgement, no timeline, no results.

Permission for my writing to be uninspired, or worse, boring and bland. Permission for bad writing, boring writing, bland writing!

The words are not who I am. The words are sent out, flavored, and brought back. To sit and simmer and brew and stew.

This waiting is cocooning. It is spiraling down and in, to the bottom / inside of me. As the world around me clashes and flashes in chaos and it feels like the coming of the apocalypse, I spiral down and in. To dark and quiet and still. To here, where there is no agenda, no grand plan, no great ambition or destination. Pulling me into the quiet, the still, the glowing dark, that is the cosmos in my womb.

This waiting, this cocooning, is important, essential. The shadow realm is vital. Pulling into a space out of time, my own internal universe. Where all that I have been and all that I am becoming is taking shape.

IF I WERE TO DIE TOMORROW, HOW WOULD I HAVE LIVED MY TODAY?

S itting in a room with other beautiful souls, participating in a meditation, I let the music wash over me. Eyes closed, heart open, the songs flowed and danced and invited me to settle deep, relax, let go.

At the end of the evening, we were invited to share some personal discovery or bit of wisdom. This was what came to me, "If I were to die tomorrow, how would I have wanted to live my today?" In speaking those words, I realized that question had become the benchmark for many of the choices I'd been making.

In previous years, at various workshops, I was prompted to write about how I would spend my life if I only had six months left to live. But I never understood the question so urgently. I always thought I had time. Time to figure it out. Time to get there, wherever *there* was.

In truth, my life was good, great even. I had most everything a woman could want. I had my family, our home, a job I really enjoyed, good friends. I wrote and had recently directed and produced "Skins I Have Worn," a life transforming experience.

Then Mike died. And my tomorrow became my today.

For months, I only had room for survival, for getting from point A to point B. Adjusting from couple to single, married to widow. It had been a long winter. But the weather was changing, spring was in the air, and with it a new sensation.

Until his passing, I loved my job, had a wonderful business colleague. We did good work, important work. Yet, after Mike's death, that work no longer called. Each day the sensation grew stronger, as I came to resist anything that was not writing, performing, expressing, or being with others talking about creativity, spirit, death and the meaning of life.

So, I gave notice to this wonderful friend, who understood and wished me well. I was a little nervous, but oddly not as afraid as I thought I would be. After all, I'd survived much worse.

I didn't know exactly what the new life would look like, but I recognized the compass points: writing, performing, nature, communion, an ever-deepening spiritual quest. Alaska sat on the horizon.

Why did I wait so long to commit fully to a creative life, a life that could light me up? Fear, doubt, comparison. Old stories about my parents, starving artists, scarcity, being Jewish, being a woman, the list went on. We all have our own, very long lists.

But as my dear friend often quoted, "The best time to have planted a tree was 20 years ago, the second-best time is now."

I couldn't go back and do it differently. I had to let go of any regrets. In fact, I had to trust that it taken the time it did because I needed to learn what I learned. Every step bringing me closer to that moment in time. Perfect.

I knew I wasn't done with the grieving. Only the day before I had a meltdown in a grocery store, collapsing into my car in bitter sobs (seems I did my best crying in the car). At breakfast the week before, I asked a friend how was it possible that I could miss him so much and yet see a future for myself that brought joy?

I felt Mike at my shoulder, encouraging me; he always wanted me to be happy. And I felt my own soul within me. Rising with a basket of flowers, tossing them across the path, dancing and laughing as I answered her call. Yes.

We are all adventurers in this thing called life. We must walk, dance, spin, leap, crawl out into the wilderness of our own lives as best we can. To our hearts saying, yes. To our lives, saying yes.

MOMENTS OF GRACE

Grace. It is one of my favorite words.
It is a word of softening, an opening. A connecting to the great Spirit.
It is feeling content, joyful, heart expanding, loved and loving.

It is holding you in my arms, my heart touching your heart.
It is feeling that in this moment all is perfect. All is beautiful.
It is a moment of time stopped. The yawn of God.
Where everything pauses for an instant and waits with hushed breath.

Moments of grace.

When we first made love.
When you put a wedding ring in my champagne.
When I held my daughter in my arms and
rocked her in the glow of the sunset.
When I stared up at the heavens and saw infinity.
When I danced, and in my dreams, I touched the stars.

When I walked into the museum and saw Michelangelo's David standing
there in all his marble magnificence and thought, there must be a God.

When you read my poems and told me you loved them.
When I stood upon a stage and let the fire burn me, hot and healing.
When I sat with you, coaxing out words, emotions, the truth.

When I stare in the mirror, hands cupping breasts,
Noting nose and arms, hips and thighs.
Staring into storm grey eyes,
Saying, yes, Dear One, you are beautiful.

DRAGON HEART

Sitting by the fire,
Contemplating the writing in the flames.
In that hypnotized state where do I travel? What
do I access with my soul's passport?

I sink into slow. Drenched in purifying smoke.
The particles dispersing so I can sink down and
down past the roots, the topsoil,
down into the sub layers of the earth.
Down further, into the boiling hot lava, the magma that is the center, the core.
Miles deep I sink until there, at the core, I touch Her.

I call her 'Her,' though she is genderless.
This is simply my imagining of a tangible self.
Sitting and staring into the heart of the Dragon.

I come and sit beside Her. It is a standing invitation no permission required.
Sit at the heart of the Dragon and stare into those blue, red,
yellow orange flames that are Her heart, our heart.

Here at the center, it all slows, stops even.
The clock as we imagine it stops moving forward.
Here we have all the time in the world to sit and be full.

Such a sense of enoughness here.
There is nothing to prove, nothing to accomplish, nothing to fear or doubt.
I am whole, accepted, loved.
My soul's heart expands to touch Hers and the flames flare and burn brighter.

For a while, eons, moments, it is delicious and perfect and deeply satisfying.

Then I feel my human-self twitch.
My nose tickles. I long to stretch my back. There
is an urge to cough and clear my throat.
My mind begins to wander to the life above. To those who
wait for me. To the garden that needs tending, the letter
that needs writing, the bread that wants baking.

I feel Her smile beside me, inside me.
Go, she nods. Though again, no permission is needed, we are free to come
and go as we please. To drop in for sustenance, nourishment, for the reminder
of who we are in our deepest places, and then to rise back up from the depths.
Reignited, rejuvenated, reminded that this is here at the core.

Then time lurches forward or so it seems, and I am back
on my couch. The smell of rising dough, the freesias in full
bloom. I hear my neighbor practicing her violin.
For a moment I feel that last lingering warmth in my chest before I rise.

THE 'WAIL' SONG

Alaska is not a place for the faint of heart, nor of body. But years earlier I'd fallen in love with the idea of it. It was a trip Mike and I were supposed to take together. Instead, I took that trip with my brave beautiful daughter by my side.

People asked how was it, what did we do? It was not the trip I imagined, but it was its own special kind of journey.

I went with no expectations, and with a surprising amount of trust that all would be well. Things fell easily into place. We found a lovely BnB with a kitchen and two bedrooms, giving us room to be together and have space apart. My daughter's friend loaned us his truck and his mountain bikes.

Oh, and he had a plane, a little itty-bitty prop engine plane.

Each one of us has our limits, our boundaries. Thanks to my daughter, I nudged and pushed mine surprisingly far, and there were truly some heart pounding moments. Though I wasn't terrified of heights, I wasn't all that comfortable with them either. But when her friend offered to take us flying in his little plane, I crazily agreed. This was probably a once in a lifetime experience.

I was numb when we took off. We lifted, almost miraculously, into the sky, heading off to the snow-covered mountains beyond, circling and flying ever higher. He was quite brilliant at calming my fears, reminding me of his years of experience. Explaining we were simply riding the currents when the plane bumped and dipped along; he had it all under control.

Eventually, I eased my death grip and was able to sit back and appreciate a view I would never have seen otherwise. At one point, we dropped down to glide over a glacier, a riverbed, and homes snuggled in green valleys of glaciers long gone. I breathed once or twice.

The highlight of the visit was a boat trip to Kenai Fjords National Park. We rode out into the open waters, invigorated by the chill cleansing air. Stared in awe as we glided past weathered mountains, thin spires of stone hosting trees and puffins, and a great tidal glacier that cracked and thundered with the constant movement of ice falling into the water.

And then there were the whales.

The captain made no promises as to what we might encounter, but even he was surprised at what we saw. On the final leg back, we spotted six whales gathered in a sheltered cove, their plumes spouting as they came up for air. Like a dance in slow motion, they'd each come up, their dorsal fins arcing over the water. Then with one final flaunt, they'd slide into the depths with a glorious showing of their tails.

For a few minutes there was nothing. The boat stopped as we watched the waters calm and the gulls settle. Waiting.

Then all at once, they rose up together. Six enormous humpback whales rose up out of the ocean, their huge mouths open to feed. They call it bubble feeding. Under the water, the whales circle a school of fish, herding them into the center and then they rise to catch them in the huge nets of their mouths. Our breaths caught at the wonder of it.

The final day was the hike up to Flattop Mountain, where from the top you could take in a 360-degree view of Anchorage, the ocean and the mountains beyond.

This was when it hit me the hardest. This was the trip we were supposed to have taken together. This was a mountain we should have climbed together. We should have sat in wonder at the peak, taken a photo by the flag, and snacked on apples and peanuts, before beginning the trek back down.

Instead, I made this climb alone. Though my daughter was with me, she was much more physically active, and I encouraged her to travel at her own pace. In a blink she was up and away moving like a gazelle, every now and then pausing to make sure I was still behind her.

So up I walked, one step at a time, trudging along at my own pace. Stopping to take a drink of water, catch my breath, appreciate the view. At times, I'd pause to stroke the moss, sniff the wildflowers, inhale the bitingly cool air. Looking up I could see what still awaited me; looking down I could see what I had accomplished.

At last, I reached the top (daughter was already heading down). The wind was stronger there; I hunkered down near a cluster of boulders to eat my apple. Then the sucker punch, I was there on that mountain top without him.

I thought of the whales, of their songs, so beautiful and mournful, that travelled for miles and miles across open seas to be heard by others. It made me wonder if Mike could hear my 'wail' songs.

Did he hear me where he was, across the unknown distance between us, maybe vast, maybe a just a touch away? Did he hear me when I wailed for him, called for him, longed for him? And if so, did he also hear me when I sighed in contentment, or gasped in wonder... or laughed in joy?

I liked to think so. I liked to believe that he was always there, a whisper of comfort and support. That he was cheering me on, step by step, celebrating the undertaking, the life I was returning to.

And I also heard my daughter's voice, her, right-here in my ear, voice. I felt her kindness and support and love, cheering me on to the top of the mountain, to the end of the trail. She inspired me to act more bravely, to be more in my body, to challenge my physical self to a greater degree. This trip brought us closer as we came to understand and appreciate each other's unique selves.

People asked me how it was, this trip to Alaska.

Wonder. Awe. Disbelief. Glory. Magic. Gratitude. Intense. Transformative.

It was a place of magical beautiful spaces. Indescribable mountains, oceans, lakes, valleys, wildlife. Time took on a different meaning there. It was a place that required great fortitude.

And I was glad to come home. To integrate what was experienced there, hold it in my heart, my body, my soul.

I could do this, I was learning. I would survive. I would thrive.

BEING REINVENTED

The in-between. Slipping down and down
into a blue lagoon of quiet.

Go deeper, go down. Into Source. Go down into the
beginning, the end. Go down into the full potential of not
just my life, but Life. The full potential of Life.

In-between is sinking into that. Letting it fill my
cells, nourish, re-form, re-frame, re-shape me.

In-between is listening, ears perked, heart open, to signs
from the Universe, from Soul. This way, come this way.

Maybe I am a snake and not a butterfly, and I am shedding
skins. Maybe I am a dragon and not a hummingbird, with eyes
swirling in reds and golds. Maybe I am a spider, not a dolphin,
weaving my web, weaving this life on central threads.

I am who I have always been. Soul is constant. Maybe she shape-
shifts some, but in essence, she is constant. Staying centered,
pivoting as needed. The spool around which I wind my threads.

But I no longer fit the same way; the skin is too tight. I am
stiff legged and tight jointed when I move. The anchors of who
I have been drop away, wife, daughter, gardener, artist.

Part of the in-between is the willingness to put it
all down. Surrender to not knowing.
Releasing attachment to all that has been known. Cutting
ropes and seeing where the winds take me.

Letting go of place, as I've known it.
Letting go of work, as I've known it.
Letting go of creating, as I've known it.
Letting go of relationships as I've known them.
Letting go of assumptions and limits, of what awaits.
Letting go of the net.

In-between is being still, being quiet, and allowing for the guidance.
Marco Polo whispers, fluttery touches of this way, this song, this step.

There is an assumption that it should be more. More potent, more powerful, more passionate, more life, more bold, more daring, more wild, more visible.

But maybe it is less. Maybe it is a simpler way of living, where my heart and body go 'yes,' that fits right, I fit right.

Less noise
Less obligation
Less responsibility
Less things
Less anxiety and worry and guilt
Less fear.

A yes that ripples along new skin. A great settling that is yes. Yes, this is it, this is me.

It is less and yes, it is more.
>More freedom
>More faith
>More love
>More connection
>More communion
>More trust
>More music
>More friends
>More expression
>More truth.

This in-between is an indefinite time when I must let go of the old, let go of the edge, and leap or slide or slip or sidle or sleep my way into my next life.

My head stops me in a panic, "But what about purpose, your gifts and talents."

Ha, toss those into the pot as well. Let them boil and bubble with the rest. In-between is the space between letting go and stepping into the "All that is possible."

I am not reinventing myself; I am being reinvented.

LET ME FEEL THIS

On the outside I am calm, cool, diplomatic, chill. That used to be high praise from my father, how kind I was, gentle, soft spoken. I'd gotten used to that, stroked by that message. You can catch more flies with sugar than vinegar.

My embers are banked.

That is the pap they sell us, so we stay calm, so we don't frighten little children. So we don't scare them or ourselves. Calm, peace, joy, all those high vibrations. Love and light and all of that.

Except sometimes I'm not that. I'm not always love and light. I am not always kind and sweet.

I am not sugar and spice because they don't really acknowledge the spice, and it's always sweetened with too much sugar.

I look at my days, how I pass the time, and ask myself what am I burning for? What does my soul crave? What is the soaring dance we are meant to be doing together?

I worked most of the weekend on a presentation about capturing water in a little can. Good material, oddly informative. But I could feel the push / pull.

Enough already. Get up. I'd been sitting all day / But I'm almost done. I'm almost there. I promised I would finish the job.

And another hour, and another hour, and another hour.

I told myself I should care, it's my job.

My embers are banked.

How do I manage this balance of soul desire and the mundane? On one hand, the desire to burn with passion, to create, to explore, to deepen and dance...

With the need to pay my mortgage, buy groceries, do the laundry, wash the dishes, feed the cat.

But I want to sing and write and paint...

And the carpet needs to be cleaned, the bedding needs to be changed, the socks mended, and I'm out of toothpaste.

I want to write about burning women. I want to be that burning woman...

But I just spilled coffee on the floor, the cat threw up on the rug, and now my toilet is clogged, and the plumber can't come until tomorrow.

Last night, I listened to a recording. I'd heard it before but had forgotten. *Just as we long to connect with our soul, our soul longs to connect with us.* She wants to feel the full human experience. The words sent shivers up and down my skin.

It made me smile to think that she might relish the impatience I feel talking to my phone company about a ridiculous bill. Is she tickled when I rage at the idiot who cuts me off on the freeway?

Does she soften when I realize I will turn 60 and my mother is no longer here to celebrate with me?

Does she curl into me, hold me gently, tasting my tears, trembling with the loss? "This, too," she whispers, "Let me feel this, too."

I turn towards her like the sun. I long to feel the burning woman. I want to burn brightly with passion and creativity. I want to embrace this life, get drunk on it. Feel the full of richness of it.

"Then brush your teeth mindfully." She says, looking at me in the mirror. "Let's take a walk around the neighborhood and see what's in bloom." Sitting on the stoop, eating breakfast, she takes my hand. "Let's sit and remember your mother for a bit, before the day takes you away."

She goes on, "There is a time for all things. Perhaps if we burn bright all the time, we burn ourselves out. And the power of the fire dulls. But that banked ember you speak of, make so little of, that ember is yours forever. To be carried anywhere, everywhere. It can be stoked into a bonfire in a heartbeat. Whenever you are ready. Whenever you need."

I feel the sun heating my thighs, the cat curling up onto my belly, the warmth of my fingers at my neck. My banked embers always there, to be stoked into a bonfire in a heartbeat.

I rest my head on her shoulder, comforted.

A New Man

I t occurred to me that at some point in the future I might want to be with a new man. Not a man who would replace my husband, but a man I could spend time with. A man who would make me laugh. A man to share meals and adventures with, and maybe the next years of my life.

When I reached the one-year anniversary, I sank into a deep wave of grief. I was struck by the terrible twin facts that I had survived a year without my husband, and that it had already been a year since he'd been gone. With the one-year mark came all the assumptions and expectations about where I was supposed to be. The bottom line seemed to be I should be getting over it by now. Moving on.

But that wasn't at all how I felt. In fact, it felt much worse as the reality sank in again, that I would live the rest of my life without him.

So, in that time of need, of choking on the sorrow, I reached out to an old friend from the past. Truth be told, we'd been more than friends. He was my first love in college. It had been a rollercoaster of a relationship. We'd lived together for a few years before parting ways, rather acrimoniously. I'd married Mike and he'd gone on to start a family many miles away.

But life has a way of changing us, molding us. At times chewing us up and spitting us out, as we continue to evolve into the beings we are.

It was so good to hear his voice. I could barely get the words out. How much it hurt, how I didn't know what to do with the emotions roiling inside of me. Not everything was grief. There were also dark feelings of anger, fear, loneliness. The sense I was standing at the edge of the abyss and falling.

Maybe one of the reasons I'd reached out was that he too, had struggled with his own dark demons. He heard my anguish and was not afraid of it. Didn't look to change the subject or pretend it was anything other than awful. In him I believed there was someone who could hold the net for me, would not let me drown. With his voice as the anchor across the miles, I could weep and share the hell I was feeling.

After a while, the ache eased, the tears slowed, and I was able to ask him about his life. He made me smile, then wrung a small laugh out of me. As I blew my nose and got ready to let him go, he asked, "Do you want me to come out? To be with you?"

"Yes, please come. Yes."

A week later we met in Denver. What a riot of emotions to see him again after all those years. I'd gotten over the first shock when I heard his voice on the phone, but then seeing him in person was another adjustment. He'd changed, of course, yet many things had not. His bright blue eyes still twinkled, his sly grin. His hands were the same as he took my bag, and my senses recognized his scent. I came off the plane, stumbling. His arms found me, wrapped around me, and held me tight, a lifeline.

I was here, he was here. I could let down, let go, for just a bit.

But it wasn't quite so simple, the grief, the transition. In the split second I said yes to meeting him, I felt relief and guilt. I knew, based on our history, our chemistry, that I was saying yes to more than a cup of coffee and a Danish. The question was could I hold both: the heartbreak of losing Mike, and the sharing of my soul, potentially my body, with someone different?

It had been a year after all. I didn't think Mike would begrudge me comfort, relief, or even a new love when the time was right. If anything, he would want nothing but my joy and happiness. But still I wrestled with the guilt. Had I waited long enough? Did it mean I loved him less?

The encounter in Colorado was strange, surreal, filled with heartache and tears, laughter and release. There was the great gift of being able to sob into a pillow and have a warm hand stroke my back. It felt wonderful to be touched, held, kissed. For a time, there was the relief of simply existing in the present moment of physical sensation and forgetting everything else that hurt.

Looking back, I was struck by certain things, odd moments that jolted me as I superimposed a new coming together against all that was lost.

The moment we checked into the hotel, no longer as a Mr. and Mrs.

He put his hand on my lower back to guide me across the street, and it was his hand, not Mike's.

Sitting across the table from him, picking at a French fry on his plate, the way I used to steal them from Mike, but it wasn't Mike's face smiling back at me.

I took his arm in mine as we stepped out for a walk, a gesture I'd done with my husband a thousand times, only this was not my husband's arm.

There are times when you walk down a path and think you know where you are going, except it is not at all the path you thought you were on. Suddenly you stumble, disoriented, it's something out of a dream, a nightmare. Your heart catches before you lurch awake and remember.

This is not the old road. This is a new road. Yet even though it is a road you do not know, the disorientation eases, the double vision blends back into one, and you move forward once again.

I saw him again, this new / yet familiar man, and there were still jolts of past and present, coffee brought to bed, cooking a meal, a hike in the woods. But with each visit, it became less jarring, new memories, different memories, were being laid down. It was no longer such a comparison.

For a time, he was friend, lover, keeper of my secrets. He was not afraid of my storms, my darkness, my tears. I did not have to pretend. He supported my creativity, listened to my rants, made me laugh, and reminded me that I was a woman, passionate and alive, with a life yet to live.

THE YEAR OF FIRSTS

They called it "the year of firsts." The implication was that it would be a painful year of all the landmarks you would have to survive without your partner: the first holidays, the first birthdays, the first anniversary, and of course, the first year after he died.

But in fact, that calendar of life after his passing was filled with firsts, an astonishing number of them. It reminded me of the calendar we kept after our daughter was born. She slept two hours, she smiled, she slept four hours (you can see how important the sleeping was), she crawled. Until, on her first birthday, she stood on her own two feet and took her first steps.

And so it was, as I traversed the terrain that was my life after Mike passed away:

> The first night I slept without the help of sleeping pills.
> The first meal I ate without feeling I would retch.
> The first walk I took longer than around the corner.
> The first week.
> The first month – somehow!
>
> The first time I woke up and his loss was not my first thought.
> The first time I made it through a day without sobbing.
> The first time I laughed or at least pretended to.
> The first time I looked forward rather than backwards.
> The first time I claimed 'My' – my bedroom, my house, my life.

The first time his death was not the only topic of conversation.
The first time his death was not in the conversation at all.
The first time I opened his closet door and did not slam it shut.
The first time I shared our memories without crying.

The first time I considered a new relationship.
The first time I went out on a date.
The first time I had sex.
The first time I had sex without thinking of him.

And so, I learned to dance again. For it was a dance. One step forward, two steps back, three steps sideways. One step, stop. Stumble, fall, get up, begin again.

Then, coming to the end of a second year without him. How did that happen? I was a different woman than I was a year ago, or even when we were married.

I was a woman, braver. For I survived one of my greatest fears come true.

I was a woman, more discerning. Having lost my love, I was much more careful with how I spent my time, aware of how limited it was.

I no longer multi-tasked, unable to drive and talk at the same time! Maybe that was a blessing.

I moved more slowly in a world that continued to accelerate. Unsubscribed to emails, silenced the phone, reduced the outside stimulation as it was too exhausting.

I heard my soul's calling more easily, more gratefully. Throughout the days I turned inward again and again, seeking understanding, guidance, at times simply survival. And in the writing, the walking, the weeping, the asking, a knowing came: an insight, a softening, a possibility, the next step.

The journey through loss is unique, devastating. But if allowed, it is a time of grace and great insight. Contradictory feelings live side by side and the pendulum swings wide as we seek to acclimate to this new reality. There is sorrow, but also an absurd humor. There is a new-found freedom to speak of things we did not dare.

There is no shortcut, no alternate route. It is step by agonizing step, as each of us finds our way to the beings we are becoming.

BECOMING

Time passes.
We move beyond the devastation.
The path continues to unfold, and
we follow the call of spirit.

Discovering facets of ourselves that would
never have been revealed had we not fallen.

Girl Unfurling

Stretching, unkinking, unhinging. Unfurling wings. Tip toes to fingertips.
The cat meows unsure of the strange sounds she makes.
Unrolling her back, unfurling her shoulders, unhinging her groin.
She grows larger as she stretches side to side.

No agenda, no story, or maybe there is a story.

What is the story of the girl unfurling her wings? In the damp forest or high
on the white cliffs of Dover. What is the story of the girl unfurling her wings?

Shoulders grow broader. She is not ready to fly yet. Everything is still so
tight, still so contained. Muscle, sinew, tendon, the right, then the left.

Who knew there were so many tiny muscles and nerves in that right
shoulder. It aches more than the left. There are more 'yesses' trapped
in the right shoulder, so many more years of saying yes, yes, yes.

No more, as the shoulder stretches to the pain and then a little
further. She rises, moves a little, this time it stretches a little easier. She
expands her chest wide. Arms outstretched. She coughs as she breathes,
fills her lungs. They are not accustomed to such deep breaths.

These deep breaths of air from the oceans, the forests, the
deserts. She is not used to so much air, so much expansion.

Girl unfurling, in the depths of the forest, the dunes of the desert,
the wildness of the crags. Stretching until it hurts and beyond.

Deep breaths, deep breaths. Of midnight moonlight and
shady glens and wild rainstorms in midsummer.

Girl unfurling, to breathe it, taste it, fly with it.

Girl unfurling, spreading her wings, ready to leap. Ready to fly.

WOMAN OF THE EARTH

I haven't washed my hair in weeks. Haven't brushed my teeth in days, feeling that film on them. I smell my armpits when I raise my arms. I like it.

The animal in me likes the way I smell. Though it's gotten a little sharper lately. My hair has become a rat's nest. My fingernails have grown brown, and you can see the lines in my palms, dark against light.

I could read my fortune in the dark lines of my palm. I bring my hand to my mouth and take a taste. It is slightly salty, smoky. There is a bit of grit that crunches between my teeth.

I am falling back into the earth. Reopening the skin, the barrier between us. I am falling back into the earth and remembering who I am. I feel the sun on my belly, my breasts, my thighs. I am pressed between the two, a menage-a-trois, held below, warmed above.
        The crevices of me fill with earth.

In the lines of dark on white there is a woman. Her body crisscrossed with inky lines, some dark and thick, some so thin it is spiderwebs on white paper. Milky globes where the ink does not stick, dark rich patches where the ink gathers.

I see the shape of her, the length of her. Notice how she stands, a slight leaning to the east and the morning sun. Her hair is wild wool with browns and reds and slivers of silver that catch the light.

What I notice, envy even, is how she stands, straight and tall and proud. There is no curving in, no sucking up, no shrinking down, this woman of the earth.

There is a circle of darkness at her navel, a pond to toss a penny into. And the yearning is so strong to touch her. To feel that skin, to trace her jaw, to bury a nose into the dips and crevices where her scent lingers.

She smiles, a deep welcoming smile. "No need to be afraid. I am no secret, no mystery. I am only unknown."

She turns slowly and each facet is revealed. The curve of her breast, the angel wings at her shoulder, the ripples of her backbone that invite fingers to dance down to the base of her spine. The rounding of her hips.

She is so beautiful this woman of the earth. What would it be to let down all the barriers? To let go of all those whispers of shame.

She turns back around slowly. No rush, no hiding. Simply turns in her white and inky form. She holds her eyes steady. "Don't be afraid. Don't be ashamed of what you want to see, touch, taste, smell. There is nothing off limits, nothing wrong."

And so it happens, from one moment to the next, I am inside, no longer outside. Free to explore.
The silver scars of childbirth, the rosy nipples, the canoes that are her collar bones. The lines that are her laugh lines, grief lines. I reach up to touch the fabric of her hair. Coming even closer, so each inhale is hers and mine.

There is a moment when skin hovers against skin, and then we are together. The ripples dance through like an electric current. The curve of my belly touching hers, softening into each other.

I nuzzle her neck, cheek against shoulder, feeling hard planes and soft tissue. Her skin is warm, and the scent of her rises like smoke, all different flavors. I could follow them back like threads to their source.

What a huge relief, a huge letting go, of so much held together, stitched up tight, wrapped up in ropes and chains and a millennium of shame.

What a gift, what a huge exhale, what an unimaginable softening it is to be with this body. In complete adoration and love. Pure, perfect.

Mine.

CONVERSATIONS WITH MYSTIC

Holding hands with soul. Touching beauty, breathing in awe. The vastness of it all held in a single drop. Indira's web and I am one of the twinkling stars. For a moment I can touch it, hold it, before it fades away.

Back in the mundane I wonder how I find joy, beauty, fulfillment in the everyday and still long for the thrill, excitement, expansion that is my "Next Thing." Standing on a balance beam, how do I live in patience and faith and still long for the universe to guide me to my next great adventure.

"Trust," a friend reminds me. "Remember. How often you have leapt when the call came. For a husband, a child, a production, a festival, a career - twice. When it is the right thing, the right time, you have always leapt."

With each breath I ask soul the question, "Is it time yet? Do you hear a tune I don't feel yet? Is there something that sets the toes tapping?"

Ripples of energy swirl up calves and around knees at this inquiry. Keep talking, keep talking. "Do I find it with 21 questions, this next adventure? Is it a place, a person?"

Soul shakes her head, "Such silliness. That bar is too low. Click-click of heels, we will go where you have not yet ventured."

Big bold soul, sweet loving soul, brave and truthful. I continue with the questions. "Is it learning an instrument? Is it a journey to a foreign land? Is it an affair with a Greek tycoon?"

She roars at that last one. "Oh, that's good."

I take her elbow, tuck my arm within it, feeling her warm skin against my cooler one. She is sister, mother, wisewoman. I cajole her, tugging. "Can you give me a hint?"

She smiles. "When the time is ripe, sweeting. It will all be clear, and you will step, the way you always have, as if it were simply waiting for you. No effort needed, no decision to angst over. It will simply be there for you, inevitable. Your path rising to greet you."

"And until then?" Sounding a bit like a sulky child.

"Until then?" She asks, almost in afront. "Until then, you live. You love. You laugh. You cry. You find pleasure and satisfaction. You find joy, delight, wonder and gratitude for this life you get to experience. For this body you are gifted to have. For these souls you are blessed to dance with every day.

Moments, big and small, are always what you make of them," She emphasizes, "What you make of them. The choice to honor and revere, rather than walk in ignorance and blindness."

There is a great calming then, a quieting, a peace. A soft exhalation.

A great adventure is in the works, the details not yet known. Maybe it has already begun, and I just can't see it yet. But faith is renewed that when the time is ripe, it will reach up to greet me, and I will step lively.

Until then, a week, a month, a year, a lifetime, I have the choice to make the most of each moment. For life is that - moments, steps, conversations, actions, wonder. This is how I am to live this life. In honor, in reverence, in gratitude.

She taps my knee. "There you go, Darling," and then winks, "But, oh, such an adventure...."

YOU MATTER

I see the sun's pale rising on the Melaleuca tree. The shadows climbing its trunk with each hour passing. With the coming of winter, I find a blanket, a scarf. Soon it will be gloves with the tips cut off. Harder to get out of that nest of blankets where I burrow my head. The dance that is too hot, too cold, too hot, too cold.

This morning I seek the poetry of me in this everyday life.

The poetry that is in all of us, making us singularly spectacular.

The old woman who keeps her cats inside while she sprinkles seeds for the sparrows.

The father who takes an extra moment with his daughter. Staring into her golden-brown eyes, capturing her gaze. Letting her know she is seen. Before a final peck on the cheek and out the door he goes.

The poetry that is two lovers sitting side by side, casually reading their papers. Yet their fingers are entwined. "I am here." They sing to each other, "I am here and I love you."

So, what is my poetry in this mundane beautiful life?

It is the surprise of a finch perched right outside my window. I watch, frozen, as it cleans itself. Fluffing feathers lightning fast in the morning sun.

The poetry of me walks in the woods feeling the trees, the green, the water. Drinking it in, longing to be a part of it. And the poetry of me that knows I am it.

> Slow down, stop, wait.

The poetry that is in a smile lifting easily to greet the day, a friend, a stranger. To let the light that glows inside flow out into the world.

It is a hug that holds you fast, holds you tight. "I've got you. You are not alone."

It is the stillness that descends when I listen to your words. A container precious and unbreakable. I am here. I am listening. You matter.

The poetry that is the stillness, the stopping, the witnessing.

> I am here, you matter.

The poetry of me pulses infinitely. But when I go too fast, my mind racing ahead of time, I miss it. When I sit on the porch thinking of what awaits tomorrow, or next week, or next year, I am missing it.

The poetry of me, of us, is in these magic words. I see you, you matter.

When I live a poetical life then everything becomes more saturated, more rich. Happening almost in slow motion. The cooking of a meal, a conversation with a friend, folding the laundry, watering of the garden.

Each action, each thought, is right there, in that moment.

An orb of you and me.

> I see you,
> Hear you,
> Feel you,
> Smell you,
> Touch you,
> Taste you,
> Contemplate you.

You matter.

We are all lights. Let me share mine with you. Let me receive yours.

You / We matter.

GRATITUDE TO MY ARTIST

Through it all has been my Artist. My Soul Sister. My Wisdom Keeper.

From the moment he died I knew she would be the one to bring me through.

> Through her I exorcised the grief.
> Through her was permission to rage.
> Through her I found a way to joy.
> Through her I felt my courage.
> Through her was the discovery of magic.
> Through her I touched awe and grace and love.
> Through her I came to understand my truest self.
> Through her I am sharing what I learned.

As I look back at the writings over those years, I see how often she was my light, my north star, my way forward. And though sometimes it seemed as if her timing was her own, she never abandoned me.

WAITING FOR NEXT

A rtist is sitting in an armchair, sipping her cup of tea. Her legs are curled up with a cozy yellow blanket on top. She is watching her sweet Girl wriggle and writhe and fuss about.

"Goodness," she says. "Let that all go. It is silliness. What are you fussing about? None of that matters. Why do you lose sleep over it, toss and turn about? It is so much simpler than you think." All of this is said with gentle teasing. Artist never speaks to her Girl with shame or shoulds. Only love. Artist speaks only with love.

She watches the spinning and clutching, the almost desperateness for that thing. The next thing. It is so simple, but the Girl she doesn't see it, not yet. Though it is as plain as the nose on her face. Funny how Artist suddenly has a bit of an Irish accent.

"Just step, and step again, and put pen to paper and step. It is nothing that is not there already waiting for you. It is nothing that must be pulled from the ether or invented from thin air. It is already there."

Artist senses the Girl's frustration, anxiety, even fear. There's a taste of fear there. That there is no next, will be no next. That she is tapped out. Has used up her quota of creativity. Perhaps that last great outpouring of grief and pain and honesty was indeed her last; she has nothing left to offer. Drained dry.

Comforting kisses, mother to child. "That is no such thing. No such thing at all. It is no different than the way your body creates and recreates itself a thousand, million times over. Cells multiply and divide endlessly, while you sleep, dream, eat, work. And so, too, does your Creative. She is in you, born and reborn, reshaped and reformed over and over again, with boundless stories to tell, poems to write, characters to discover.

True, there are times when you Girl, are tired and tapped out, drained. You need the pool to be refilled. There are times when the tide is out, and inspiration needs a nap. But she never disappears. We are not the apple we are the tree. The source is infinite."

Artist sits back and takes a crunch of a biscotti, this one dipped in chocolate, and another sip of tea, waiting and watching.

The Girl raises her hands to the heavens, slips to her knees to pray. "Where is it? My next. What is it? My next." She calls on her guides and angels and seeks desperately for the wink of inspiration. She peeks around corners and stands all tense, shoulders hunched, waiting to feel the mystical nudge.

Artist wants to laugh, kindly, of course. She thinks it's a bit like the Girl is constipated, trying to push it out. Trying to force 'next' to appear.

Each time we go through this. Girl is better this time, patient longer, more willing to trust her process.

Girl slows, drops her hands and sighs. It is exhausting. Pleading to the muse, to inspiration, who feel like petulant children. The more she chases after them, the faster they run. Laughing all the way.

Artist watches more carefully now, waiting for the moment. It is coming. She can feel the swirling of energy slow. The chaos, the rushing about, the chasing and pleading, coming to stillness. The particles drift and glide about, landing at last.

Girl takes a deep breath, remembering. We've been here before. This is what happens when we lose trust and faith. She has forgotten for a time this is innate. It comes to her the way breath does. It is the blood coursing through her body. It is dizzying images that appear suddenly, the way words jump in front of the pen. The delicious plots that unfold on paper like cobbles on the road. Like water flowing from a stream. But only when she lets go of chasing it.

Until then, the earth continues to turn, the tides roll in and out, and when the time is ripe, whatever is growing and becoming inside of her will make itself known. No need for darts at the target, no guessing games, no picking a name from a hat. When it is time, it will present itself on her doorstep, like a long-lost friend, hat and cane in hand. "Are you ready, Darling?"

A huge grin lights up her face as she reaches for the crook of their arm. She welcomes her Next with a certain amount of relief and steps out, her feet pitter-pat.

Artist smiles, a deep contented smile. "There she goes, my lovely Girl." Artist finishes her cookie and takes a last sip of the tea. Then rises from the couch, uncurling herself like a giant cat.

"There," she laughs. "That wasn't so hard."

THE BEAUTY OF SLOW

I feel the pressure to write something. Not just any something, but something brilliant, insightful, true. My props are here, paper, pen, coffee. I wait for inspiration.

Yet, as I sit here, I smell the double crown daffodils in the vase next to me. I feel the ache in my lower back, even with the stretches and exercises. I hear the heat come on and off. There is an underlying hum I don't notice until the refrigerator turns off.

If I were to go slow, I would notice this. If I were to go slow, I would discern the layers upon layers, into infinity, of what surrounds me and pulses beneath my skin.

The taste of coffee deliciously brewed with whole milk. A touch of honey to sweeten the bitterness. The sound of the pen overlayed by the rumbling of a two-prop engine droning by. When I raise my arm, a whiff tells me it is long past time for a shower.

Slow is the invitation to now, to being attuned and focused. Slow is the invitation to details. Not broad strokes of red, but the thousand gradations of pixels that make up that color.

A flash of light is a car driving by. There is a bird singing in the tree in front. Somehow, I can tell the difference in direction between a bird in front and a bird on the side.

Slow is the ripple of cricks as I move my neck from side to side. Imagining what happens as I use muscle, tendons, to move spine and head an attempted

45 degrees. As it reaches its edge, I feel the tightness, almost pain. No further.

Then the breath deep into the lungs as this belly expands. As it calms and sooths the muscles, the nerves. As my neck releases and eases just a little bit further.

Slow is an opportunity to expand, to go beyond. To ease, ooze, through time and space.

Slow is how I am learning to salsa. It's in the details. Not just where the foot goes, but how the balance shifts. The way my hand and his hand move together in synchronicity.

Slow, and again, slow, as my brain and my body put things together. As my brain struggles to remember and my body begins to retain it.

> Slow. Again slow. Again slow.
> A little faster now. Again.
> A little faster now. Again.

My body and brain begin to tag team. We are still counting steps, but it is coming. Less thinking, more moving. Until it isn't thinking any more. Until it is there in the body.

Faster, now. With music, now.

Feeling the breeze as we whip to the right, or spin to the left. The delight as arms add a little drama, as hips add a little sexiness. As I meet his eyes and we smile at our success. As we delight in the fact that we are doing it. We are dancing.

The moment when slow paves the way for delight, for joy, for expansion.

So as much as I would love to get to the next exciting part of my life, I think of the beauty of slow.

How much there is to appreciate in slow.

And how, ultimately, slow is the way I will get there.

SPIRAL

Do we think it goes away, grief?
Just because 'enough' time has passed.

That we should be over it by now.
That it doesn't still catch us by surprise

When we see an old couple sitting on a bench
And think: That should have been us.

I Still Miss You

It is 2 ½ years, November 8, and it still aches. Not the rip
me apart, devastated way it used to. But it aches.

I miss you. I miss your face, your way of being, your habits, yourself. Your
solid, I've got your back, self. Your funny quirky self. Your "I'm turning
into a pumpkin, let's meet at the farmers market," soccer-watching self.

I miss the "Let me treat you to dinner" self, your camping,
moto-hiking self, your own self, your own sweet self.

There is no one to come home to. No one to share adventures
or stories or annoyances or celebrations with, the little and big
things. No one to sit with on the swing, watching the sun set.

The question still comes up, how do I do this, this life without you? I
am amazed again how much I love you, loved you, miss you. I didn't
understand when others said at three years, five years, eleven years, it still
hurt sometimes. I didn't think it was possible and here I am missing you.

Is it still 'grief'? No, not in the "I can't breathe" way, the "I can't think of
anything else" way. The black void that swallowed me whole, leaving nothing
but confusion and sorrow. It is not that anymore. But it is something
today. My voice catches when I speak of you. As we come around to the
holidays again. A third time. You are still the missing limb in my heart.

It is not so much a matter of what I do, for I am doing it. I am living a
life, filled with highs and lows, celebrations and regrets, laughter and
pleasure and frustrations. My pages are filled with accomplishments, big
and small, choices made. I am assimilating to a world without you.

There is a vision suddenly. You rise from the ocean, surfing up from the depths to give me a kiss. Reminding me you are there, never far away. It is a gentle kiss on the cheek as you glide along like a dolphin beside a boat. Swimming next to me, with me, and yet out of reach.

Then you dive down, slip out of sight. Off on adventures of your own, adventures I am no longer privy to.

This time, I do not flounder, fall apart, tumble to my knees. I wipe my tears, blow my nose, and rise to begin another day.

STORY OF A RING

M ike told me the diamond on my ring was Montana mined, found in those mighty Gallatin mountains. I'm not sure if that was true, but I loved the idea of it. He gave it to me one night, slipped it into a glass of champagne when we went out to dinner. I watched through glistening tears as the bubbles floated to the surface in the glow of the candlelight.

Several months later, the day before Cinco de Mayo, he put that ring on my finger and told me how much he loved me. We stood on the Palisade Bluffs surrounded by family as we took our vows. I was worried some police officer would come by and tell us we were not allowed to get married on public property, so, we were stealthy in scouting out our spot. Then finding it, the perfect place by a circle of rose bushes, we stopped and gave ourselves to each other.

For 28 years since then I wore it nearly every day. On occasion, I took it off for a massage or digging in the dirt. Every day, all the time, I would touch it, fingering the gold, twisting it about my finger. When I was cold it moved easily, when it was hot, it was harder to shift.

Towards the end of my grief support group they asked if we still felt "married." At the time, I thought the answer was no. I didn't feel married the same way I felt when we were together. And yet, I hadn't taken off the ring.

On occasion I tried. One day I was gardening and took it off, placing it safely on my dresser. I thought I would test it, leave the ring off for a while, ween myself from it. But once my hands were clean, my finger felt naked. I could feel myself searching for that missing piece like a blind woman.

I could see the white band against my darker skin, a puzzle needing to be complete. "Where are you?" They called to each other, my finger, his ring, "Where are you?" And quickly, quickly, I slipped it back on. Relieved.

But then at two years, a voice, not my own, whispered "Isn't it time? Isn't it time to take that ring off, to let him go?"

I considered the possibility that by keeping this ring on, I was showing the world, and any potential partners, I was still committed to another. How could I possibly invite another love into my life when I wore this ring as my protection?

I considered what I would do with the ring if I took it off. I could place it in a velvet lined box and put it on my dresser. I could give it to my daughter on her wedding day. I could put it on a chain and wear it around my neck, close to my heart. There, and yet, not there.

But then my finger, my heart, shouted out "Not yet! Not yet!" I realized I didn't have to take my ring off, not then, maybe not ever. In that moment it was not necessary, there was nothing to prove.

HOME IS SIMPLE

"Where is Home? What is Home?" That was the prompt from a writing class.

Initially, when I thought of home, I heard the phrase, "Going to the underworld." I liked the sound of that, it felt important, almost a chant. "I'm going to the underworld." But my voice creaked and cracked so I walked away from that.

Then I played with tossing 'Home' in the air, seeing what might happen if I went beyond my typical forays. Home was where I could finger paint on the wall, splash mud on the floors. Home was feeling free to eat chocolate cake with vanilla ice cream, using my fingers to dip into the sweetness. Sensual, pleasurable, maybe even erotic or wild.

But all of that felt a bit forced. So, I began again and discovered that when I didn't try so hard, home was actually very simple.

Home was a warm blanket and a cup of coffee, that first taste. Home was paper and pen, where I could share and discover whatever was in my heart. Home was that sacred safe place where I could be utterly myself. Home was very simple.

It was where everything outside, all inputs, were turned off. The noise, the news, the voices. And with that, the fears, the doubts, the expectations, the stories. All turned off.

Home was my couch and the morning light. That magical time when all was still and quiet, before I let the rest of the world in. The birds calling to each other, the cat curled up behind me on the pillow.

Home was very simple. It could also be under the canopy of a great oak, where I smelled the pungency of the chaparral, heard the soughing of the wind. Taking in great big breaths, taking it all into me.

Home could be the seaside, where I was hypnotized by the sounds of the ocean, in and out. The gulls crying out, the magic of dolphins leaping in the water. While I simply sat there, curling my toes in the warm sand.

No worries, no obligations, no misunderstandings, or tense relationships. No fears about climate change, or droughts or school shootings. No sorrows, no illnesses, no horrors around every corner.

Home was quiet and still, and I was not pulled apart or harangued by all that noise. Home didn't need fancy wallpaper, marble floors, or infinity pools.

Home was in the garden eating a tomato and cucumber salad. Feeling the crunch between my teeth, tasting the sweet salty flavors of my meal. The sun at my back, the splash of the fountain, the cooing of the doves.

Home was where I was simply myself. Relaxing into permission to feel whatever I did: joy, grief, love, anger, inspiration, excitement, sleepiness. Where I could hear my own voice, sweet, pure, true. And I could hear hers, my beloved soul. Speaking in a language we had developed for a millennium.

Home was looking up on a dark clear night and seeing a billion stars above, winking in and out. Breathing in that cool crisp air, and knowing to the deepest part of me, that this was all Home.

As small as a seashell, as huge as the Cosmos.

Home.

SAFE HARBOR

I n the beginning after Mike died, there was nothing but chaotic indescribable heartache. Telling the story of what happened over and over again, as days, weeks, months passed. Simply surviving.

As time wore on, and the intensity eased, I found it liberating to talk about death. I welcomed the invitation to talk about Mike, what happened to him, how I was adapting to life without him. I was also aware of how I looked at loss around me differently.

One thing that struck me as odd was a perceived hierarchy to loss. As if somehow one kind of loss was more significant, more valid, than another.

More than once, when someone shared a story of loss, they'd preface it with, "I know this isn't the same as losing your husband…" Of course it wasn't. But that didn't make it less painful, or less important. It was still a loss. There was still grief.

A friend of mine was going through a nasty divorce and felt guilty about burdening me with her feelings. True, I wouldn't have had space for it in the beginning, but with time, I could hold both. In fact, it felt good to listen to her, feeling more compassion than I might have in the past. Able to share what I was learning, offering threads of hope as she navigated her own path.

Then there was the phrase that triggered so much emotion, "I understand. It's just like when I lost my …" The offence taken, the temptation to draw the grief up around us like armor. Believing there was no deeper pain, no greater loss. And to us that was true.

As it was to the one who had lost their friend, their sister, their precious animal.

It is time to let go of comparison and judgement. There is no need to one-up the greater loss or grief.

Let us be free to mourn as we need to - mother, brother, friend, pregnancy, partner, home, child, cat, grandfather, the planet.

Let us not compare which was worse. That we knew they were dying or that it came as a shock. That they died of old age, illness, accident, flood, fires, shootings, suicide, misdiagnosis.

The list goes on and on, all the unlived promise, all the unfinished business, all the time we thought we still had. And now don't.

Throughout it all, I believe we can be safe harbors for each other. We can listen with kindness and compassion to someone's sorrow. There is no need to "fix" anything, for in truth we cannot.

But it is a gift beyond measure to be witnessed, to be held.

To witness, to hold.

Just because my husband died doesn't mean I can't hear what your sister meant to you.

I am delighted to hear stories about your grandfather's adventures growing up.

I love laughing with you as you tell me how your cat found you.

My heart aches with yours as you share the loss of a pregnancy. Or how you honored your son when he was killed in Afghanistan.

I will pour a glass of wine as you tell me what it was like driving up to a home no longer standing.

I will sit on the porch and cradle you as you re-read the last letter you received from your daughter.

Let the words be a gift; they are appreciated. As are the arms that hold, the hearts that soften, the ears that listen, the eyes that glisten.

Speak of them, share them. This is how we honor them, remember them. This is how we nurture the love that doesn't die.

THE REVOLUTION

I am unfolding other parts of me.
Writing a new reality.
Inviting in wild magic,
Infinite possibility.

Wondering…
Who could I be beyond the grief?
What would I call in?
How brave might I become when I remember what I survived.

SNAKE

It only hurts for a moment when she strikes. Her fangs sink into my wrist. The venom hot and cold as it runs like a river through my bloodstream. In moments it hits my heart, and it is like riding the rapids. Pulsing with each beat into arms, legs, brain, womb.

"There." She smiles, if snakes could smile. "There." As everything goes still. The quieting of thoughts. It is just her and me. She almost purrs as she shifts her belly on the rock. She is all belly. Moves both slow and fast.

The initial panic at the numbness start to ease. I can feel my stomach, chest, warming as we meld together on the hot rock. I hear her inside of me. "I am curiosity, invitation. I am transformation."

I want to coil my neck the way she does. "I am infinite capacity." I feel a giant opening inside, as if I have swallowed the cosmos. She is the cosmos. Our bodies entwine in infinite capacity. Disappearing into the smallest of cracks, expanding to swallow a lion. You don't mess with Snake.

"Solitude. Alone but never lonely. Potently self-sufficient. I am solitude. Feel the steadfastness of that, the groundedness of that. Don't be afraid. I am infinity. Swallowing my tail. Where do I begin? Where do I end? Where do you begin, where do you end?

Going back to the very beginning, stretching out to no end. The DNA that flows from the very first cell will continue to the very last. You are alone and yet infinitely connected.

No need to fear me, my quiet power. Not roaring like my Sister Lioness or howling like Cousin Wolf. They move differently in the world, on four legs, making lots of noise. I do not need to be loud to be heard. I do not need claws to be deadly.

That fascinates you doesn't it, my poison. We can protect ourselves. They cannot hold us if we do not want to stay.

Your mind struggles like the mouse to understand. They are right to be afraid of what they do not understand, what they cannot control."

"Why do you shed?" I ask. "What is that gift?"

"It is how easily I leave the past behind. I do not carry it with me like Sister Turtle. Such a load she carries, but she has her own medicine.

It is transformation, evolution, change. I am change. Welcome it. The old gets itchy and tight and I can't move with as much agility. It holds me back. So, I strip it off like a hot shower that sends dirty water running down the drain. Carrying with it yesterday's thoughts, fears, accomplishments.

Each day we are in a different place. It may seem as though nothing has changed, but that river is endlessly flowing. Your cells change. You are becoming again and again, though you may not be aware.

Welcome the evolution, Sister. Welcome the ever-changing you. Welcome the power of your solitude, the power of your poison, the power of you."

After a bit, I become aware of our dissolving connection. I feel her twitching in my body as I unkink from our time together. I turn around to look at her, she has settled her head up on her coil and lowered her scales to sleep.

Wondering if I imagined it, I touch my wrist and feel the two points where she pierced me.

Unlikeable

Unlikeable, unreliable, undependable, unbelievable. The great unraveling, like a top spinning, as the string releases.

This letting go of accolades and gratitude and pats on the back for a job well done. Unpredictable, changing colors and shapes and sounds. You think you know me, but you don't.

A great hurricane blows through, stripping me of past, of history, of assumptions and expectations.

Until I am left newly born.

So, let's roll baby, with Unlikeable.
Madame Unlikeable to you.

She takes no shit. Says what she thinks.
Does what she pleases.
Apologizes for nothing.

She doesn't pitch her voice too high, too soft.
Doesn't end each sentence with a question.
She is bold in her speech, pulls no punches.
Diplomat she is not.
No worries about hurt feelings
Or saying the right thing.
She stomps on eggshells.

But she is all in.
No hedging her bets,
Gaming to be on the right side, the winning side.
She doesn't dance to applause or criticism.
She doesn't play coy.
She doesn't bat lashes or fans.

She is who she is.
Sleeps when she's tired,
Eats when she's hungry,
Fucks when she's horny.

She doesn't patiently wait, while the soup gets cold.
She eats with gusto, with pleasure.
No worries about counting calories.
She embraces her wrinkles, her bags, her lumps and bumps.

This is all me, this is the life I have lived.
I am wearing the life I have lived.

She feels pleasure deep and rich,
Wallowing in warm mud, like a pig in a puddle.

She puts herself first.
Boundaries are strong with a "don't fuck with me" line.
Your shit is your shit, and my shit is mine.
Takes no responsibility for what is not hers to carry.

Sovereign being, Sovereign woman.
Bows her head to no one, no man, no king, no authority.
She is not awed by wealth or celebrity.
We are all equal under the sun.

She is not afraid of loud,
Of foolish,

Of anger or conflict.

She does not accept everything, just because they say it is so.

She will not be abused.
She will not be taken advantage of.
She will not be hidden – behind a door, a man, an expectation.

She knows what she likes and stands for it.
She knows who she loves and stands for it.

She is daring and brash.
Makes mistakes and keeps going.
Pisses people off and doesn't care.
She sings and dances and plays the piano badly.

She is not afraid to fail.
She is not afraid to succeed.
She is not afraid to be seen.
She is not afraid to celebrate or feel joyous.
She is not afraid of grief or sorrow.
She is not afraid to love or trust, full out.
Big breasted, wide arms, I love you, Darling.
Full mouthed kisses under a lamp post.

She doesn't always keep it together.
Sometimes she flies off the handle, a wild banshee witch.
She embraces Bitch.
She embraces Psycho.
She embraces Nutcase.

Bring it on baby, she shouts to the crowds.
She is not afraid to swear.
She doesn't hide or pretend.
What you see is what you get.

No apologies for who she is or what she does.
No cowering, or embarrassment, or shame or pretending.
There is no playing of games.

She is rock solid, waterfall wet, bonfire hot, hurricane winds.
Whoosh.

Funny, as I come to the end of this writing, I
am aware of what I label "unlikeable,"
        a woman who is herself.

TASTING GREEN

I decided I wanted to get away for a month, a real sabbatical. Leave Los Angeles with its traffic and noise and a pattern of living so ingrained. At first, there was excitement, a month away. Living a different life than I had ever given myself permission to experience.

Then I got scared and panicked. Maybe not a month, but two weeks, or one week. Or maybe just stay home. Piggily wiggly running all the way home.

But then, taking a deep breath I stepped back to the source of the invitation. To live a life fully, to get drunk on life. There was nothing I had to prove. No badge of courage I needed to earn. This was for me and my soul. With each breath, I let myself sink into a vision.

Sitting by a creek, the day warm and the waters cool. The tumbling of those waters quieting the noise in my head.

All around, it is so green. The colors are intense, dark greens and bright, forest greens and emerald. The floor of the forest is thick with mulch and new seedlings. The sun passes through the branches casting a kaleidoscope of shadows on the ground.

I watch the waters for tiny fish, water skaters, even crawdads. Spider webs glisten with dew. Everywhere life is happening.

I am my senses.

Smell. Did you know the day smells differently depending on the time? Morning, afternoon, evening, as the sun warms the trees, the soil, the moss, my sweat.

Sound. My ears are tuning forks turning this way and that. Of course, the water, but even the water is not one sound. There are many threads of water that tumble over this rock and around that one. That catch on a branch, lift into the sky, and then land as 100 different little percussive hits on the shallows below.

Beyond the water, tuning into the forest behind. The branches touching each other with the breeze, insects buzzing, birds conversing. The beating of my heart.

Deeper still, to the Earth herself. The sweet inhale and exhale of the great Mother. I find that my breath moves into sync with hers. Big deep inhales and slow, such relief, such letting go, exhales.

Taste. I stumble at that. I wouldn't dare taste; it might be poison. Though as a child I had no such fear. I used to eat dirt. What if I let go of fear and trusted taste?

The water is cool and fresh with a hint of algae and stone. I lick the rocks, run my tongue over smooth and rough surfaces. Taste salt and ancient life. I feel the crunch of tiny particles between my teeth.

I go on relishing this adventure in taste. Onto the greens. Some are delicate like a blade of grass. Some are tart, many bitter and hard to chew. There is the occasional blossom I bite only with permission; the most delicate of petals melt on my tongue tasting of vanilla and honey.

I've enchanted myself with this writing. The fears dissipate. The fear I might get lonely or bored. The fear I might find myself pacing a room, seeking escape in television or a book. Afraid to be with myself without stimulation.

But I hear my soul whisper, "You have yearned for this forever. You have called it in. The wind has heard and answered. Now, my Love, now is time to journey."

Towards the Rising Sun

I t is a big deep breath of chilly air that sparks me awake after what has felt like an endless slumber. I'm lacing up my hiking boots, buttoning my jacket, wrapping my scarf. Setting out into the woods.

The day is bright and sunny, crisp and exhilarating. My life feels invigorating, though I don't know what to do with it yet.

Maybe that doesn't matter. In this moment, all that matters is that my sap is running, I am alive, and it feels good.

My pack is filled with a sleeping bag and tent, jerky and dried meals. There's a canteen and water purifying pills. I have my walking sticks; they were Mike's. I step out onto the path and close the door. I have a map, the old-fashioned kind made of paper, and a compass.

This morning, I am heading east towards the rising sun. Towards new beginnings. I have been in the cave a long time. In a near-endless winter of hibernation, moving like molasses. But the ice is cracking, the snow melting. Buds are forming just below the bark. Not yet visible, but there.

Setting forth on this new adventure, I don't know what it is yet, how it will manifest. I don't know what buds are just below my surface, waiting for their time to leaf out. But I am ready, willing, inviting.

Curious as to what trail will appear as I let go of the past, as I cut the line that keeps me safe and predictable. What is the song I want to warble to the trees, howl to the fire? What is the dance I want to share with the creatures of the woods?

I am moving into the forest, letting go of what I have known, what keeps me comfortable, complacent. I am stepping into unknown,

> Different,
> Unkempt,
> Wild,
> Wondrous.

I like that, stepping into wild, wondrous.

A step, and another, further away from the house I've known, the couch I've worn curves in. The television I have allowed to comfort me, while keeping me asleep for all this time.

A bit of anxiety flares up at that thought. What will I do without that television, as the sun sets and the sky grows dark. As I am left alone with myself and the flickering fire.

Letting that go, I feel my heart pound and my cheeks flush. The sun is almost glaring in its brightness. I stop and listen for the sounds of the forest. The aliveness that is all around.

> The quail running underbrush, the hawk keening above.
> The crackling of branches in the wind.
> Quieter still, the drops of snow melting and falling to the ground.
> The rush of a creek in the distance.
> The hesitant peep of birds that dare to come out when I am still.

It's alive, it's all alive. I breathe deep, shift the pack on my shoulder, and step out.

East, towards the rising sun.

LOVE WAITS

She sits in a corner. Young, maybe four or five. In a dark blue dress. She is tucked deep in that corner, protected by walls on two sides and the floor below. She will not move from that corner where it is safe. In a world where suffering is part of the human condition, she will not leave the walls.

Just beyond is a woman with a wounded heart. It is covered, protected, sealed with wood and iron, welded shut. She would like to be happy but has forgotten how. She is tired of putting on a mask and pretending.

Delicate fingers trace the iron, the wood. Kneading, massaging, softening, around the container that holds that heart so protectively.

Love.

Heart stiffens. The protection hardens. "You can't come in," Heart whispers. "You can't come in."

Love's fingers continue to stroke gently, as though coming upon a wild animal. Letting it get used to her smell in bits and pieces.

"Then I will wait with you." Love slides down the wall, not in disappointment, not in anger, only in patience. "I will wait for you, with you, as long as it takes."

The young girl in the blue dress watches for a while. Then, in a moment of impulse, rises and joins Love, sitting down at the base of the wall beside her. They reach for each other's hands.

"We have a lifetime if you need it, if you want it. We will wait."

Against the wall, Heart feels the warmth come through. In her own moment of impulse, she leans against it, Love just on the other side.

Love and the little girl are singing now, harmonies and melodies and notes that rise up and down. Heart can't see them, but she can hear the music, feel the vibrations through her body, making her feel warm and safe.

Love is gentle and kind and so very compassionate. She will not push. And Heart is sad, so terribly sad. "It's ok to be sad," Love whispers. "We don't think less of you because you are sad." She sings on. "We are just outside, feeling and loving your sadness."

Heart curls up inside, while Love and the girl sit outside, hugging and singing sweet songs, Love songs, for Heart. "Until the sun rises in the sky and the moon circles the stars, we'll be here for you."

"Me, too," the girl sings out, "Me too." So much braver now with Love at her side. "Me, too. I'll wait forever."

And Heart, that darling, sweet sad heart, curls up against the warmth of the wall, soothed to sleep by the songs of Love and the girl, just on the other side.

* * *

I wondered if that was where I would end the story. Not pushing, just waiting. There was nothing wrong, it was simply where we were.

Then, the sun rose in the sky and the moon circled the stars and Love waited while Heart slept and healed.

And there it was nestled in the story, **time**. *For Love to wait patiently through all time as Heart mended in the safety of Love's embrace.*

There will come a time when enough healing has happened, when the cocoon that Heart needed to mend will no longer be necessary. When she will no longer feel so hurt and sad.

And when that time comes, she will step through the walls into the arms of Love and the little girl, and they will laugh and cry, dance and sing, all in each other's arms.

BECOMING WINGS

Blue, green, gray.
Wild woman stands at the ocean's edge,
Finding comfort there.
The sounds endless. Crashing.

"Breathe deep, Little One." The voice rolls in with
the foam. "Breathe deep and let go."

Cold water against toes. Sinking into wet sand. Sun on shoulders.
Eyes closed to the glare.
Listening and holding on so tight. So very tight.

"Breathe deep, Little One." She hushes again.
A seagull cries as it circles above.

Knees softening, hands dropping, head falling, sinking in.
Deeper and deeper.
Breathing.

"Let it fill you. Let it go." Caressing skin.

Wild curls flutter around a face, tears dripping.
Salt meeting salt.
Soft. Stay soft. Let it come.
The waves crash at her feet, splashing knees, wetting skirt.

Lost now in the sounds, the caress.
Arms lifting to feel the wind.
Becoming wings.

Bio

We are, none of us, just one thing, but rather glimmers and glimpses of so many things.

Marianne was brought up in a household of artists, surrounded by writing, music, dance, and theater. Over the years, she performed on stage and television, began directing plays, and ultimately started writing her own. Her writing expanded into essays, stories and poetry.

In a surprising detour, she discovered a passion for nature and went back to school to become a landscape architect. It was a completely different form of expression, and yet similar.

Along the way, she raised a beautiful daughter and shared a wonderful life with her husband until he passed away.

Finishing this book is the closing of a chapter. As she steps into the next phase of her life, she is embracing it with joy and anticipation.

Visit https://www.mariannebecoming.com for more.

www.ingramcontent.com/pod-product-compliance
Lightning Source LLC
Chambersburg PA
CBHW030105070426
42448CB00037B/968

9 781732 143616